Shine

Discover your inner sparkle, do work you love, and light up the world.

Michelle Keating

Founder of Dreamers Collective

GLOW AND GROW PUBLISHING

Shine: Discover your inner sparkle, do work you love, and light up the world
Author: Michelle Keating

Published by Glow and Grow Publishing
Auckland, New Zealand

michellekeating.com

Contact publisher for bulk orders and permission requests.

Copyright © 2025 Michelle Keating

Cover & book design by Michelle Keating and Leesa Ellis of 3 ferns ➢ 3ferns.com
Cover & book formatting by Leesa Ellis of 3 ferns ➢ 3ferns.com
Self-publishing consultancy by 3 ferns ➢ 3ferns.com

No part of this publication may be reproduced or distributed in any form or by any means, other than for "fair use" as brief quotations embodied in articles or reviews, without prior permission from the author.

The views and opinions expressed in this book are those of the author, based on her personal experiences. This book is intended to provide inspiration and general guidance, however, readers must consider their own circumstances before accepting the opinions of the author and applying them to their own circumstances.

The author makes no representation as to the suitability or validity of the content of this book to the personal circumstances of the individuals who will read the book. and will not be liable for any errors, omissions, loss, damage or claims arising from the contents of this book. In the event that you use any of the information in this book for yourself, the author assumes no responsibility for your actions.

Printed in the USA.

ISBN (Hardcover): 978-1-0670581-0-4
ISBN (Paperback): 978-1-0670581-1-1

CONTENTS

A note from the author 1

CHAPTER 1   Do more of what makes you happy 5
    Falling out of (cupcake) love 5
    Heaviness 10
    The good ol' days 12
    Hunting for happiness 15
    How stationery stopped me in my tracks 16
    Hip-hop happiness 19

CHAPTER 2   What's the work you can't not do? 25
    Redefining work 25
    Climbing the right mountain 28

CHAPTER 3   The Messy Middle 33
    Tug of war 33

CHAPTER 4   Inner Grit 41
    Building my conviction 41
    Becoming a B-School butterfly 43
    The beginning of the end 45
    Change for good 47
    Dressed for Success? 52

CHAPTER 5   A leap of faith 57
    The problem is me 57
    Afraid to stay put, but terrified to move on 59
    Bali to the rescue 60
    Embracing Grace 62
    Taking the leap 65
    Ready to Shine 71

EPILOGUE 75

JOURNALING EXERCISES 93

How to use this section 93

Do more of what makes you happy 95

30-day Happiness Challenge 96
Happiness Board 97
Happiness Jar 100
Happiness Habits 102
Create a motivational playlist 103
Journaling 104
    Stream of consciousness journaling 104
Surround yourself with inspiration 105

What's the work you can't not do? 107

Values 118
Strengths 123
Extra resources 123
    Value Determination Process 123
    Trombone Player Wanted 123
    CliftonStrengths® Assessment 123
    My favourite TED Talks 124
Bringing it together 125
Light up the world by being you 128

The Messy Middle 131

Remind yourself of your destination 132
Speak your new reality into existence 133
Your support crew 134
Quieten the 'what-ifs' 136
Re-energise yourself and build your belief 138
My List of Inspiration 139
    Books 139
    YouTube clips/channels 139
    Movies 139
Review your current situation 140
Practice gratitude 145

Inner Grit 149
- Meditation 150
- Setting a deadline 151
- Commit to your success 152
- Write a letter from your future self 153
  - A note about investing in yourself 154
- Make time to work on your dream 155
- Learn from others 158
- Role models 163
- Peers and finding your village 164
- Mirrors 166
- Dealing with disappointment 169

A leap of faith 173
- Getting unstuck 174
- Leap of faith checklist 176

Final words of encouragement 179

Keep in touch 180

Acknowledgements 181

About the author 183

There is a uniqueness within you, an inner sparkle. When you connect to it and have the courage to share it with the world, you'll experience the magic of being lit up from within. Now is your time to Shine!

A note from the author

Hey lovely,

I'm imagining what brought you to **Shine** is a feeling that there's something more you're meant to be doing with your life, yet you're not quite sure what that is or perhaps how to get there.

Maybe you're wrestling with frustration, a feeling of "Is this it? Is this all I am capable of?" You're longing to know what it is you're meant to be doing but you can't quite put your finger on it. And try as you may to ignore it, that feeling just won't go away.

Perhaps you're tired of moving from job to job only to end up dissatisfied or you've tried and failed at doing something you love. You worry you're settling for something less than you're capable of but you're afraid to try again. Or perhaps it's a niggling feeling that you're missing something important. Whatever it is for you, I want to let you know this: that feeling is your greatness calling you. It's the part of you that knows deep down that you're destined for more and it wants you to experience it.

How do I know this? Because I had it too and for the longest time, I chose to ignore it. But I knew I needed to start listening as there was definitely something else out there for me and I wanted to find out what it was.

Shine is about listening to your inner wisdom and doing the next right thing to build and live the life of your dreams. As we learn best through stories, through lived experiences, you'll hear my raw and real journey of moving from a job I could no longer stand to pursuing the life of my dreams. I take you through my journey of self discovery – the fear, desperation, and many, many bumps along the way, to show you that pursuing your dreams is within your power. And even if it's not a straightforward linear journey, that's okay.

You'll read how I've pushed through my perfectionism, embraced being a beginner, got curious about what ignites my passion, stopped avoiding conflict, and put my faith in something only I could see and feel.

As this is a story of my personal experiences, the interactions I describe are from my perspective. Some in particular were clouded by my internal struggles, so I have therefore chosen to omit names. I am and will always be eternally grateful to the beautiful souls who helped me see what I had previously been unwilling to look at, so I could be guided to discover my own inner sparkle.

> *My experience taught me that being myself and pursuing a life of purpose wasn't just meant for a select few. All of us have the potential within us to create and live the life of our dreams.*

Yes, that means you too.

The journal section will not only help you listen to that small voice within that's been telling you you're meant for something greater, but I'll also take you through the steps to confidently walk your own path towards the life of your dreams. Consider me your guide along the way. I'll help you get started with clarity and confidence and guide you through any scary bits.

You can choose whether to complete the journal activities as you go or after you've finished reading my story.

Whether you've had this feeling for five minutes or five years, trust me when I say there is something on the other side worth going after.

There is a uniqueness within you, an inner sparkle. When you connect to it and have the courage to share it with the world, you'll experience the magic of being lit up from within. It is a 'money can't buy' feeling that opens the door to joy, lasting fulfillment and a sense of purpose that will help you navigate any of life's challenges, while knowing you are on the right path.

Shine is my gift to you – because the world needs your unique sparkle.

It's your time to Shine!

Michelle x

You have everything within you to design and live a life you love, one that's a reflection of who you truly are.

CHAPTER 1

Do more of what makes you happy

Falling out of (cupcake) love

Growing up in New Zealand, I thought I knew how my life would unfold from an early age. It was the tried and true path – go to school, get a university degree, start a career, climb the corporate ladder, get married, buy a house, have babies, go on overseas trips, and I'll be happy.

So I worked hard at school, got good grades, and followed the expected path which led to a career as a graphic designer. After my fair share of disaster boyfriends and some awesome overseas experiences, I met my now husband Rob and by my early 30s, I thought I had finally ticked all the right boxes (minus the babies).

I'd secured a full-time graphic design role which had allowed Rob and I to purchase our first home together. The next step was marriage and then onto babies. Tick, tick, tick off the list of life achievements.

We enjoyed a beautiful wedding in 2011, a project that had filled me with great joy. I loved coming up with ideas of how to decorate the venue, what details to include on the invitations, and the special touches such as displaying the past wedding photos of our guests at our reception to celebrate weddings through the decades. I had been in my element. I listened to wedding podcasts, pored through Pinterest and bridal magazines. I created a magical wedding day. But once the festivities were over and my creative outlet was gone, I started to feel flat.

Something started to feel off at my job. I was beginning to wonder where the promised happiness was. Why did I feel empty inside? Everything on the outside looked in place, but inside something felt out of place.

The feeling was something like the movie 'Pleasantville', starring Reese Witherspoon and Tobey McGuire, where everyone is smiling, appearing happy in a black and white world. They've been sold a dream where doing all the right and expected things brings an ideal of happiness, yet for many inhabitants of the town, life was grey. It's not until Reese and Tobey's characters enter the world and start introducing ideas and experiences that bring colour into people's lives that they realise what they have been missing.

I couldn't help but feel I was missing something, but I didn't know what it was.

Initially I brushed it off, putting it down to post-wedding blues and looked for something to distract myself. At the time, cupcakes were in vogue. I began teaching myself to decorate cupcakes and became obsessed. Before then, I'd never made a batch of buttercream before and only remembered the ugly marzipan wedding cakes with their thick almond icing on hideous fruit cakes.

I found myself experimenting with all kinds of different cupcake designs.

I ordered supplies like they were going out of fashion. I studied YouTube clips of decorating techniques and found joy in surprising my friends, family, and colleagues with intricate creations, like cupcakes decorated to look like they were a bouquet of flowers covered in petals and arranged in a pot. I spent hours piping each individual petal until it was hard to tell the difference between my cupcakes and a real flower.

People would routinely tell me they looked too good to eat and ooh and aah over my creations. I became so obsessed that I started counting the cupcakes I baked and finding any excuse to bake a batch. I surpassed the 1,000-cupcake mark within a year.

My husband even surprised me with a fancy countertop mixer for Christmas and I squealed so excitedly. You may have thought I'd been given the winning lottery ticket or the keys to a new car with a bow on it.

> *My talent and passion didn't go unnoticed. People started telling me that I should start a business selling my cupcakes. Initially I brushed it off, telling them I had been in business before and wasn't very good at it, so I didn't want to do that again.*

I had run a business in my early 20s as a fairy princess entertainer. It had stemmed from my time spent working at and experiencing the magic of Walt Disney World in Florida during a university summer break. That and the fact that I've always loved sparkles and my best friend at the time was a ballet teacher. I came up with the idea to take a break from graphic design and become a children's birthday party entertainer.

I literally had no experience. I put up a flyer at my friend's ballet school and before long I booked my first gig. Unfortunately, the birthday girl had no idea I was coming and burst into tears when she saw me. It went downhill from there as I soon realised my inexperience with young children meant that the games I had planned were not age appropriate for the party guests. I struggled to gain control over the crowd of 4-year-olds who seemed to be more interested in making noise and twirling around than following my in-depth instructions for the complicated games I had concocted.

Somehow I survived and went on to refine my show, and at my busiest, was booked every weekend for a year. I was in my element. I declared I would never work for anyone else again. I was even invited to be the fairy princess on top of a float in Auckland's biggest Santa parade. As the giant swan with two younger fairies perched on the top slowly made its way along the streets of the central city, I smiled and waved to the kids and their families in the crowd of thousands of people. Each time I caught the eye of a child and saw their joy and excitement of being acknowledged by a real fairy princess, it made my heart swell. In my mind I had made it to the pinnacle of 'fairyness' – being the fairy princess of Auckland.

But, despite my passion and hard work, I didn't manage to build the business in a way that was financially sustainable. I was living at home practically rent-free with my parents, and despite the joy that I had given children and their families, I wasn't in a position to look after myself. Eventually, despite other indicators of success, like happy clients and word-of-mouth referrals, I decided I should go back and get a 'real' job.

I had just met my now husband, Rob, and working weekends at parties started to lose its appeal. I found myself a design job and initially felt pleased to have money rolling in which allowed me to move out of home into an apartment with a friend. There were many benefits to being employed so I dismissed Princess Cinderella parties as a phase. Even though I had gone back on my word and had become an employee again, I justified my decision saying I was doing the right thing by building a solid career. Clearly, I deduced from the experience, I wasn't cut out for running my own business.

But as more and more people nudged me to consider starting my own business making cupcakes, I couldn't help but think, could I do it again? How could I do it in a way that didn't jeopardise my family income and the stability we had? I'd convinced myself that I was a failure in business. I'd even removed my entertainer experience from my CV to avoid embarrassment when applying for 'real' jobs.

Surely I shouldn't try that again and risk another failure? The question kept circling around in my head as it became more and more obvious that I was more passionate about baking cupcakes than my day job as a graphic designer.

The answer to my internal dilemma came to me through Gok Wan's autobiography, **Through Thick and Thin.** If you're not familiar with Gok, he's a UK fashion stylist extraordinaire who shot to fame as the host of his own TV programme, 'How to Look Good Naked.' He is known and celebrated for his incredible fashion sense, stylish glasses, and uncanny ability to help women feel beautiful and confident in how they dress.

Through Thick and Thin is Gok's backstory of his life before he became recognised around the world. I was enthralled by his account of his painful experience growing up as an overweight Chinese boy who found comfort in food, only to later become anorexic. He felt like he failed at everything, only to realise that his experiences gave him empathy to relate to the insecurities of the countless women he helped to regain their confidence.

His remarkable story struck a chord with me. I thought to myself: Wow! Out of all that failure came something so beautiful.

Gok's story lit a spark of courage within me. Maybe I should give this business thing a go again. Maybe this time I could turn my talent into a viable business and leave my 9 to 5 job for good. Perhaps that would cure this feeling of emptiness about my job. I began dreaming of making cupcakes while raising a family and how much freedom and creativity that would give me.

I was determined to do it differently to the Princess Cinderella parties. This time I would make a profit. I was going to make it work this time.

I carefully worked out costs for my ingredients and felt like I had made the perfect plan to leave my day job for a life of making cakes. I got a Food Safety certification, found a local kitchen to rent and started to spread the word. I had my new business: Cupcake Love.

Word got out and the orders started to roll in. I made hundreds of Valentine's Day cupcakes and Mother's Day bouquets. After one wedding order, I got the most incredible phone call, as the mother of the bride expressed that they were the best cupcakes she'd ever tasted.

I worked late at night during the week and worked on weekends. I spent the better part of two weeks intricately constructing perfect miniature replicas of the Muppet characters. And my carefully created cat and dog cupcakes were awarded runner-up for best cupcake in the annual SPCA Cupcake Fundraiser Day in 2012.

I began telling friends how I was ready to let go of design. And I'd found something I'd never felt more passionate about. There was a real sense of conviction that this cupcake business was the thing.

Then a familiar sense of dread started to creep in. I was about ten months into Cupcake Love and the wheels started to fall off. Despite the hours and hours I had dedicated to my craft, once again when adding up the hours I was spending on the designs, the numbers didn't match up. My hours spent didn't equate to what I was charging for my orders.

Despite all the hours, all the courage and creativity, even the many happy customers, I found myself in the same place I was with my previous business. I'd hit the same hurdle. I was indulging my love of creativity, but the finances weren't where they needed to be. I was in no position to leave my graphic design job.

I began questioning my ability. One night while out for dinner with friends, I recall feeling judged by one friend. The subtext of what she was saying felt something like: "Oh, here you go again Michelle, chasing your dreams and not getting ahead."

She probably didn't intend to hurt me, but it exacerbated the thoughts I was already wrestling with. I'm working hard but I'm not succeeding, again. There must be something wrong with me. I was good at baking. I was good at coming up with creative ideas. I watched other people succeeding in their businesses and thought that this business was supposed to be easy. And because it's not easy for me, it must be my shortcoming. I'm really not cut out for self-employment.

I was home one night baking an order after a full day of work. Elbow deep in icing, Miley Cyrus' song, 'The Climb' started playing on the radio. As I listened to the words, tears started streaming down my face.

Scan to listen to the song or visit michellekeating.com/shinemusic

I didn't know how to fix what was wrong. Everything felt impossible, the mountain of living my dream life in business didn't feel climbable at that moment.

My inner critic started popping up cruelties like: How could you be so stupid? Everyone else is better than you. You're never gonna make this work. Why did you bother trying all those things? It's weird having these ugly, heavy thoughts when you're baking and decorating something pretty and delicate like a cupcake.

From that moment in the kitchen, I started to check out of Cupcake Love.

Heaviness

I began to put more boundaries in place, calculate orders more carefully, track my time and charge more. But it felt too late. And my passion wasn't there anymore. Orders started dwindling as a result – which felt like a self-fulfilling spiral.

Losing hope wasn't black and white or overnight. The best way I can describe it is energetically things dried up. It felt stale and heavy.

Potential clients would start asking me, "Do you do this kind of service, this kind of cupcake?" and I just started saying, "No, I don't." Not surprisingly, Cupcake Love completely ended shortly after that.

The end of Cupcake Love felt like the end of the dream to run my own business. For that to be gone, it was heartbreaking.

I hung up my apron on that dream.

I was envious of people who I'd seen make it and felt the embarrassment of having done it again – and failed. I felt like a defeated gladiator, face down in the arena with everyone in the stands jeering and laughing at me.

A real sense of despair set in around my job. I began thinking: "Is this all I'm capable of?" I had mustered the courage to have another go at business and yet here I was again, and it felt ten times worse this time.

I piled on the self-criticism and expectations – "But look, you've got an income, you are paying the bills. You should be grateful. You should be happy" Soldier on and get on with it, basically.

But, of course, I wasn't happy.

The fallout of Cupcake Love was touching every aspect of my life. My whole demeanour changed. The realisation my 9 to 5 was all I had made me feel like I was dragging myself into the office. The voices in my head would drum into me, "You should be grateful." But I didn't feel grateful. I felt horrible.

I had been promoted to Team Leader of the design department and the wider marketing team needed me to do things on time; but I would miss deadlines. They needed to be kept in the loop; I'd not keep them updated. They needed me to be reliable; I was saying all the right things but not following through.

I'd overpromise and underdeliver and brush it off when they asked me about it. I'd say things like, "I'll get round to it" but I didn't.

People were losing trust in me.

They didn't hide their disapproval. But I was so down, I was carrying the failure of Cupcake Love. Every weekday, I was in an environment where everything was making me feel worse. Some colleagues would talk to me in an angry tone which would trigger even more unhappiness and outrage in me. I was so wrapped up in my own unhappiness that I'd put it back on my colleagues.

I began bitching about my job and colleagues outside of the office to friends, family, and anyone else who'd listen. I put on a fake smile in the office, but I silently fumed at my desk.

I had so desperately wanted to do my own thing, to live that dream, yet all I felt capable of doing was a 9 to 5 job. I felt resentful and hopeless. Why were other people able to live their dream lives and not me?

To help escape my misery, I turned to something that always helps me gain clarity and inspiration – music.

The good ol' days

I turned to the old rock songs I listened to as a teenager. Listening to them made me feel nostalgic and comforted. Those songs took me back to a time when life was simpler. Growing up, I loved going to concerts and following bands, sometimes waiting in line for hours to buy tickets and hanging around outside after the concert for a chance to meet the artists.

One of my favourite bands is the Foo Fighters. I first saw them live in 1996 when I was 14 years old. I lined up with other eager fans at the doors to the venue hours before they were set to open and was lucky enough to sneak backstage for a few minutes to meet lead singer Dave Grohl. Every time I've seen them live since, which is at least 5 times, I've always been amazed at the energy Dave has.

I searched for their song 'These Days' on YouTube and watched the music video. It showed Dave saying goodbye to his wife and children as he goes off to play shows around the world. The video footage cut between different shows, and then I noticed something familiar. One of the shows in the video was the concert I had been at in Western Springs, Auckland, in December 2011.

Scan to listen to the song or visit
michellekeating.com/shinemusic

Watching that video, looking at the lead singer Dave Grohl at the very same concert, I felt this connection. I thought to myself, "That man is doing what he was put on this earth to do. He gives absolutely everything, and I can feel it when I'm in a stadium with him."

I contrasted the feeling of being in a stadium with Foo Fighters to how I was feeling sitting at my desk. I don't want to be a rock god, I thought, but I wouldn't mind being my own version of that, a version where what I do makes me feel as alive as that. A critical voice piped up in my head, saying, "Yeah remember, you tried and look where that got you".

Reminded of the despair I was feeling about not feeling joyful about my job, I kept going down the list of bands I had loved growing up and landed on Everclear, another of my favourite bands when I was a teenager. Again at 14 years old, I begged my parents to let me go to their Auckland concert after seeing them play and meeting them at an in-store appearance. It was pure joy rocking out to their pop-rock songs.

Now, decades later, I stumbled across their new album release, Invisible Stars. Listening to new songs with the same familiar sound instantly lifted my spirits. I felt like a teenager again and loved their new music as much as the music they had released when I was younger.

After work, I went onto social media to tell the band how much I enjoyed the new album. It was late by the time I got to my car so all I could see was the glow of my phone screen against the darkness around me. I found their profile and before I hit the message button to contact them, I noticed their most recent post. There I saw an announcement that Everclear would soon be touring New Zealand.

My eyes widened and I took a second look. I couldn't believe the synchronicity. It had been years since I had seen them play, and now, just as I needed something to lift me out of the heaviness I was feeling a literal light in the darkness was in front of me. I knew I had to go.

They were performing back-to-back concerts – one was a private acoustic concert and the other was a larger concert. I bought tickets for both – I felt like a giddy teen again and it was so exciting. It gave me a good distraction from my work woes.

The acoustic concert was small and intimate in a little bar in Auckland's Parnell. Given the band hadn't been in the mainstream for years I didn't know anyone else who was still a fan, so I went along by myself. I got chatting to other super fans like me in the queue and we shared stories about our love of their music.

I told them about the time when I was a student working in the USA over summer, I went to the Santa Monica Pier, which is the name of one of Everclear's biggest hits. I got Mum to bring over the album cover from New Zealand when she joined me for that leg of my trip so I could get a photo of me on the Santa Monica Pier holding the album. A couple of friends shared how they did something similar. They drove to a place called Summerland when travelling in California, the name of another of Everclear's songs – that's when you know you are among true fans!

As we took our seats near the front and waited for the band to appear, I felt that familiar rush of excitement when you know something good is about to happen. When lead singer Art Alexakis took to the stage with the band, and they played the first notes of songs that I'd played on repeat as a teenager, happiness flooded me and a beaming smile spread across my face.

The band played a mix of old classics and songs from their newly released album. Art shared stories I'd never heard about their songs and afterwards, instead of heading backstage, he came and talked to us. The friends who had traveled to Summerland got to meet him for the first time and I was overjoyed to be able to soak in their absolute elation of finally meeting their musical heroes. We were all giggling like school kids and fizzing like over shaken soda as we lined up to have our photo taken with the whole band. This was just what I needed, I thought to myself, a reminder of what it's like to feel good.

I arranged to meet up with the other superfans at the larger concert the next night, because of course we had all bought tickets for both. Being up the front at the live concert on Auckland's 'K' Road made me feel like I was 14 again. I stood in the crowd in my favourite bright coral jacket, with its three-quarter-length sleeves, soaking in the energy as Art and the band played hit after hit for the enthusiastic crowd.

As the set came to an end, they played one of their earlier songs, 'I Will Buy You A New Life.' As I listened to the chorus, time stood still for a moment.

Scan to listen to the song or visit michellekeating.com/shinemusic

I thought of my corporate job and how bad I was feeling and thought: I want a new life, yes. Buy me a new life. A life where I get to do something I love, just like the musicians I admired.

The lyrics to that song became a mantra of sorts. Something was starting to shift within me. I knew things needed to change. I didn't need to feel this bad. I was starting to gather the energy to do something about my situation.

Hunting for happiness

The Everclear concerts gave me the lift I needed. The lyrics I heard and the message I felt in them stayed with me.

A few days later, in another moment of serendipity, a little magic and insight happened. I was upstairs at home with our two cats, Charlie and Mynx who were on the bed snuggling on our chocolate brown mink blanket.

I was forever taking photos of the cats and I snapped a photo of Charlie – my cat who loved snuggles. In the photo it was clear that he was purring – happy and content. A random thought popped into my head – what if I look for something that makes me feel happy every day in November, take a photo of it and post it on my Facebook profile?

There was a candid photo from the first Everclear concert that one of the other fans had snapped of me taking a selfie with Art which had been making me smile whenever I looked at it and this photo of Charlie was making me feel the same way.

Without giving it too much thought, I started my Happiness Photo challenge. The purring picture of Charlie was the first photo I posted.

> *I was going to look for the good, instead of feeling bad about how things were. I started scanning my environment for the good, for the joy, for the things that actually made me happy. It was both a mindful activity and a gratitude exercise.*

My focus was simple: find something that signified happiness and joy to me, photograph it and share it. One day it was the line-up of my favourite shoes and the next it was the sign on a Glengarry wine shop, because well, wine makes me happy! It didn't have to be deep and meaningful, it just had to be personal and intentional.

I wouldn't end a day without finding something that made me happy. By the end of the month, it felt like I'd had a major reset and shift in my perspective. Friends had started commenting and connecting with what I was doing. It gave me a sense of purpose beyond just surviving at my job. I moved from "I hate my life" to "How do I become happy?" It's almost like I had been running on empty but I started to fill myself up again.

I started questioning things – What would happiness look like to me? What is my version of happiness?

The answer, it seemed, would come to me through a stationery store.

How stationery stopped me in my tracks

One weekend, I was browsing in my local mall, in Takapuna, on Auckland's North Shore, looking for a present for my sister. Something caught my eye in the window of a store. I looked up and saw it was the stationery company, kikki.K. I recognised the brand having had colleagues in a previous graphic design job who loved purchasing their beautiful stationery items from there. I had dismissed the brand, as I assumed kikki.K just sold expensive stationery.

At the time, I would rather have spent my hard-earned money on shoes – but something about the window display drew me into the store.

If you've never been in a kikki.K store, the crisp white shelves that lined the store were the perfect backdrop to the array of different stationery items, all lined up neatly in rows. Watercolour motifs, inspiring quotes, and simple but beautiful Scandinavian designs with lush textures drew me in further. Nothing was there by chance or accident, everything was there by thoughtful design. I felt like I had wandered into an oasis of serenity. As I moved around the store, I settled on a display of journals with words like, 'Goals' 'Happiness' and '101 Dreams' on the cover. The sales assistant must have noticed me being enthralled, as she came alongside me and shared the story of the kikki.K brand.

I picked up the 3am journal as the sales assistant told me the story of Kristina, the kikki.K founder, and how she woke her partner up at 3am in despair, not knowing what to do with her life.

Her partner encouraged her to write down her dreams. This simple act changed her life and led her to create the global stationery brand.

To experience the beauty of her dream brought to life, I thought, "Wow! If she didn't know what she wanted and she went on to create all this, maybe there's hope for me."

At the till, a new stationery item in my hands, the salesperson handed me a flyer and told me about the workshops they ran in the store. One of the upcoming workshops was on Happiness and included a copy of the journal I had just been admiring. I was intrigued, given I had just started focusing on what made me happy. But, as the workshops were held at 10am on weekdays and I worked full-time, I thought: Well, that's a shame, that time doesn't work for me.

But I took the workshop flyer home anyway because it was home to a quote that struck a chord: "Don't let yesterday take up too much of today."

I decided to put it on the wall in the office. I strung up a piece of twine and used little wooden pegs to hold the quote in place. That humble piece of twine became an extension of the happiness challenge I had started with my Facebook posts. I began to add other items that sparked joy in me. The leftover cupcake topper from an 80s day at work with a photo of another of my favourite musicians

Jon Bon Jovi on it and a photo of my friend's adorable twin boys were just a couple of examples.

That quote and that moment in the store came at the perfect time. It gave me permission to think maybe I could do something different. It was the reminder I needed that it was okay to make mistakes and that I should not let the past hold me back.

Before long, I became a regular visitor to kikki.K. Whenever I was in a suburb with a kikki.K store, I'd go and browse the new collections and purchase another stationery item. Every time I walked into the store it felt like a sanctuary. Somewhere I could go and be surrounded by positivity and the belief that it was possible to do something amazing with my life. During one visit, I picked up a postcard from the counter that was advertising their happiness workshops with the saying, 'Do More of What Makes You Happy' in beautiful watercolour on the front.

To keep me inspired, I put this postcard on my desk at work.

Over the summer break, my happiness quest got taken up another level. I had been browsing social media and spotted the idea of creating a happiness jar. The idea was to write down something that made you happy on a piece of paper each day and add it to a jar. It seemed like the perfect way to continue what I started with my happiness posts. I committed to making 2013 my year of doing more of what made me happy. It felt like a far cry from the misery I had been consumed by only a couple of months earlier.

I must have told my manager Kimberley about the kikki.K workshops as one day she was smiling broadly at me when I sat down at my desk in the morning.

"Guess what?" she said. "After you told me about the kikki.K workshops, I registered my interest last time I was there. The Britomart store just called me to let me know they are holding a Happiness workshop in the evening, should we go?"

"Ummm...yes! Of course we should," I replied, giddy with excitement that I could continue to add to my recent experiences of happiness.

A few weeks later, Kimberley and I were sitting in the Britomart store. We had our brand new Happiness journals on our laps, grinning from ear to ear as we listened intently to the workshop facilitator take us through how to build and sustain happiness in our lives. One exercise in particular grabbed my attention. The facilitator shared with us the importance of creating 'happiness habits'. Regular, intentional activities that bring us genuine joy and allow us to be present in the moment. She encouraged us to find things that brought out our passion and make them a priority.

For a brief moment, while watching the facilitator, I thought to myself: Maybe I could lead workshops. Before I shrugged it off and concentrated on the session, I let myself daydream a little about what it would be like to do something like this on a daily basis.

An added bonus of attending the workshop in the evening was having the store to ourselves to purchase items that would compliment the happiness journey we had just embarked on. Of course I left with a few more new stationery items, as well as a feeling of excitement to complete the journal we had started.

Journaling was a new experience for me. I'd kept a diary when I was younger, but I hadn't answered questions in a structured way before like the journal contained. It was eye-opening. There was something special about the clarity I gained from writing my thoughts down on paper and exploring my happiness. It was like with each word I wrote, I was giving myself permission to really own what made me happy, not what I thought should make me happy.

I kept the Happiness journal and some coloured pens on my bedside table. On weekend mornings, I spent time working through the sections and prompts. I was keen to continue my Happiness journey and found a much greater awareness of my thoughts when I saw them written down on paper. I'd never experienced the clarity of answering specific questions and uncovering my own personal thoughts on happiness, some of which surprised me. Through journaling, happiness went from a vague concept to something I had more control over than I thought. Journaling became a habit I would return to time and time again because of the depths of insights I was able to uncover.

Hip-hop happiness

With the idea of happiness habits fresh in my mind, one day I turned up at the gym unusually early for my regular Les Mills BODYPUMP™ class – one that uses weights and helped me look and feel fabulous on my wedding day.

I walked up the stairs to the exercise studio and caught the tail end of the previous class.

As I entered the room, an energy hit me like a lightning bolt. The room was filled with at least 200 people, music was pumping, and the studio lights were flashing. Enthusiastic gym-goers in fluoro gym tops, baggy pants, and high-top shoes made up the majority of the people in the room. Everyone was dancing in-sync and seemed to be having the time of their lives.

I looked to the front of the room to see who was responsible for the electric energy and saw the instructor on stage moving with an incredible precision and energy that radiated off him, it looked like he was glowing he had so much passion for what he was doing. I couldn't take my eyes off him and felt myself being pulled into the vortex of the energy coming from him and in the room. It felt so good and I wanted to be part of it.

I thought to myself, "What's going on? Who is this person? This is what happiness feels like and I want IN!" The contrast to how I was feeling in my daily work life felt like night and day. Being witness to someone with so much energy radiating off them and being in a room filled with so much unbridled joy felt like the storm clouds parting and the first rays of sun shining through.

The instructor was Gandalf Archer Mills and the class was BODYJAM™, a dance based workout. Interestingly, I had tried BODYJAM™ before, back in 2010, when I first joined the gym to get fit for my wedding. I had tried most of the classes Les Mills offered and had done one class of BODYJAM™. I had immediately decided I was never going to do it again. I'd felt hopeless, uncoordinated, and embarrassed because I couldn't follow the moves and felt like everyone else was better than me, a feeling I didn't like in the slightest. I'd left feeling defeated, wrote it off as a bad experience and had focused my efforts on classes that required less coordination, like BODYPUMP™.

This time, however, I felt drawn to Gandalf's energy. My focus on happiness inspired me to ditch my BODYPUMP™ class the following week and nervously take myself along to Gandalf's class. Dressed in my usual exercise regalia of tight lycra bike shorts, a singlet and running shoes, I felt out of place amongst the fluoro-clad, high-top wearing regulars, but I didn't care. Something told me I needed to be part of this.

Just like the first time I tried BODYJAM™, I was pretty terrible. I turned the wrong way to everyone else multiple times and barely got a move right, but having the opportunity to be around the energy of someone doing what they love was worth feeling like a fool. I left feeling uplifted and couldn't wait to come back for more. This, I decided, would become my happiness habit.

I became a regular at Gandalf's Wednesday evening and Saturday morning classes, gradually transitioning from my traditional workout gear to brighter colours and baggier pants and tops. It would often take me weeks to learn one routine. But the experience of being in a room filled with good energy kept me going through the moments of frustration of not being able to master the moves right away. When I eventually nailed a routine, I'd leave feeling on top of the world. The classes became about so much more than just exercise, they were another oasis I could come to shake off the internal feelings of failure and despair I was grappling with. I'd be concentrating so hard on what I had to do that it was a break from all the internal negative chatter in my head.

I had discovered something in my life that I could joyfully fail at. Failure used to feel like the end of the world; I'd be so hard on myself. But dancing became an activity where I could safely slip up – I could let go and enjoy the process, rather than obsess over a perfect outcome. Showing up to Gandalf's classes and giving myself permission to do the steps wrong was a huge milestone for me.

> *Like Art Alexakis and Dave Grohl, it was clear Gandalf was doing what he was put on this earth to do. But more than that, their love for their jobs had an innate reciprocal joy. By doing something they love, other people experience a deep joy too.*

It dawned on me, perhaps doing what you love is not selfish. Once you've found and live your purpose and share it with others, you inspire and benefit other people. Dreaming – and living the life of your dreams – becomes an act of generosity.

I was ready to put the failure of Cupcake Love behind me. I wanted to discover what my reciprocal joy was. What was I put on this earth to do?

Ready to do more of what makes you happy?

You can pause here and go to **page 95** to complete the journaling exercises for this section.

Note to self:
This is not about changing who you are.
This is about <u>being</u> who you are.

CHAPTER 2

What's the work you can't not do?

Redefining work

This shift in thinking led me to look for more positive things to distract myself from my continuing frustrations about my job. My happiness practices had helped lighten my mood and shift my attitude toward things, but I was still struggling with the tasks I didn't like doing and the tension between myself and my workmates.

On my drive to work and while sitting at my desk I started to listen to TED Talks. The short, inspiring talks by a variety of people from around the world available on YouTube presented a different view of work than what I was experiencing. Titles like 'How to Know Your Life Purpose in 5 Minutes' resonated with me as I continued to ponder the question: What was I put on this Earth to do?

I found one by Scott Dinsmore entitled 'How to Find and Do Work You Love'. He started off his talk by taking in the experience of being on the stage and uttering the words, "I was wondering what this would feel like", clearly thrilled to be on the TEDx stage to share his thoughts and ideas. I listened to him share his experiences of leaving unfulfilling work and building his own movement 'Live Your Legend', a career and connection platform to inspire people to find their passion, that grew to help over 30,000 people around the world. His words made me realise that I had been conditioned to think that you are supposed to hate your job, that the misery I was feeling was normal, and that most people felt the same.

Scan to watch Scott's TEDx talk or visit michellekeating.com/shineresources

He recommended becoming a self-expert and working on understanding yourself, explaining that when we understand what is important to us and what our natural strengths are, we can make career decisions that embody who we are. I was listening. I had already begun to uncover what made me happy, perhaps this was the next step for me to take, to find out more about what made me tick.

How many movies and television shows had I seen that centered around the misery of being at work? It was an accepted norm – do something you don't like, get paid, and look forward to weekends and holidays.

Listening to Scott got me questioning everything I believed about work: What if I could not only like what I do but even love what I do? What if I could find work I really enjoy? He finished his talk with the question, "What's the work you can't not do?" There it was again, said in a slightly different way: What was I put on this earth to do? I became even more determined to find out.

Then a friend recommended I listen to some of Dr. John Demartini's talks. Dr. Demartini is a world-renowned human behaviour expert who has helped thousands of people master their lives and find their purpose through his education curriculum, many books, and seminars.

Dr. Demartini's philosophy is about discovering your values and aligning your life with them. He talks about living by your highest values to become your best self and doing what you were put on this earth to do.

I started immersing myself in Dr. Demartini's material. He became another voice in my ear that backed up what I had just heard from Scott Dinsmore – you are not supposed to hate your job. I heard story after story of how he'd helped people uncover what they valued most and design lives that were a reflection of their most aligned selves.

I looked up the Demartini Value Determination Process online and answered a series of questions like 'How do you spend your time?', 'What do you spend your money on?', and 'How do you fill your space?', all designed to uncover what you are naturally drawn to and value the most. I looked around my space, clearly inspirational quotes and stationery items were high on my list of things I valued! I was being drawn to beautiful things, but why? I reflected on my choice to become a graphic designer. Maybe I'd thought becoming a designer would mean I would spend my days creating beautiful things, when in reality the majority of what I was doing in my current role was not that. Perhaps the tension I had been feeling and experiencing with some of my workmates was partly the result of an internal tension within myself.

Maybe it was one of the reasons I was feeling so miserable. I wasn't living in alignment with my values. I had 'borrowed' the values of society that said, "This is what will make you happy". But my 9 to 5 role wasn't making me happy at all. I wanted to explore this further, maybe it would lead to some answers about what I was meant to be doing.

More help came via my older sister, Anna, who had recently moved to Canada to complete a life coaching certification course. Having heard me complaining about my ongoing work struggles, and having put herself in an environment where she gained access to lots of coaching tools, she sent me a link to a video series by Marcus Buckingham called 'Trombone Player Wanted'. It told the story of a kid who was expected to play the trombone at school, but he was naturally drawn to the drums. No matter how hard he tried to focus on the trombone, he kept getting distracted by his interest in the drums. It wasn't until he found someone else whose eyes lit up when she picked up the trombone, the same way he did when he played the drums, that he was finally able to switch instruments and be content.

Through the videos, I began to see that just because you're able to do something, if you feel drained after doing it, it's likely that you're not playing to your strengths and it's even more likely that you'll never truly enjoy it. I began looking at my role at work in a different way. There were parts of it I enjoyed, mostly when it came to big picture thinking and dealing with people in a positive way, yet there were also things that I struggled with, following through on the repetitive, mundane tasks and dealing with difficult or aggressive people.

I invested in the CliftonStrengths® Assessment that was referred to in the video series and also in Scott Dinsmore's TED Talk. My top five strengths came out as WOO (Winning Others Over), Positivity, Communication, Futuristic, and Strategic. As I read through the descriptions of each one I found myself nodding in agreement and recalling examples of when I had felt aligned with them in my life. It made sense why I felt energised when connected with new people and why in my current and previous roles I could spend hours strategically designing processes. It explained why I would sometimes freak out when major changes to our design work, such as brochures or packaging, were suggested because I could intuitively sense how a small change could affect all the different artwork versions and take hours to execute.

It was beginning to become clear to me that while I was 'good' at graphic design, it didn't light me up completely, so no wonder I was feeling stuck and miserable. But what else could I do with my life if design was all I'd ever seemed to be able to make a decent living doing?

Climbing the right mountain

I was excited by the possibility of doing something more aligned, but it still felt like an impossible task to piece it all together and hold it together at work. The more I became exposed to alternative ways of living and working, the more desperate I became to figure it out so I could get the hell out of my situation.

I embraced the help of my sister again when she offered the opportunity to be one of her coaching 'guinea pigs' so she could practice the skills she was learning in her coaching course. During one coaching session I visualised myself climbing up the side of a snowy mountain, like Mt Everest. Yet, off in the distance, I could see another mountain. I desperately wanted to be on that one instead of the one I was on. What a waste of my time and energy! Here I was scaling the graphic design mountain, even though I didn't want to reach its summit. It was the perfect metaphor for my situation. No matter how much effort I put into climbing the mountain of graphic design, it was ultimately fruitless as I didn't want to be on it.

It was time to get off that mountain and onto one that was meant for me.

Soon after, I read an article about Walt Disney in an issue of a magazine I'd been drawn to while out grocery shopping with my husband, The Collective Hub. I'd loved hearing the story of how The Walt Disney Company started during my induction to work there as a university student. Except this article was different, it told the story of how Walt's first business attempt, Laugh-O-Gram Studio, had failed and he'd filed for bankruptcy. Say what?! I'd never heard that part of his story before. I was left with this overwhelming sense of gratitude that Walt didn't give up after his first failure. What a massive loss it would have been if he hadn't picked himself up and tried again. If Walt had given up, the world wouldn't have the Disney films, characters, and theme parks that generations of children and adults have adored.

I had a sudden realisation: What if Walt's bankruptcy was the learning experience he needed to figure out how to make Disney successful? What if what he learned from his first experience had helped him build a stronger business later on?

Did that mean the same thing might apply to me? What if my previous perceived 'failures' in business were actually stepping stones? If I never tried again and resigned myself to a 9 to 5 job for the rest of my working life, would the world miss out on something that I had to offer?

A wave of certainty came over me. I realised that if I was truly honest with myself and put aside my feelings of failure from Princess Cinderella Parties and Cupcake Love, I would rather spend the rest of my life trying to figure things out in business, than spend the rest of my life working for someone else in a 9 to 5 job, wondering whether I could have done something amazing.

Yes, I said to myself. I do want to be in business. I want to use my failures as learnings and stepping stones to success. I made a vow to myself to this effect. Even if it might take the rest of my life to master it, I knew the mountain I wanted to climb.

Ready to discover the work you can't not do?

You can pause here and go to **page 107** to complete the journaling exercises for this section.

Every day is one step closer to living the life of your dreams.

CHAPTER 3
The Messy Middle

Tug of war

From the moment I visualised my right mountain, I wanted to do everything I could to build a bridge between where I was as a graphic designer to where I wanted to be – a woman thriving in business.

Unfortunately, I couldn't just effortlessly abseil down the wrong mountain and then miraculously summit my dream mountain. It wasn't a case of just making the decision and resigning the next day. I had to go through the 'messy middle' that so many of us would rather avoid.

The next few months that followed was an unrelenting tug of war. Yes, I was being pulled by my vision of a better, happier life, but I was also pushed back into my old ways of thinking by fear and doubt. It wasn't enough to just have the dream play in the background. I still felt desperate, craved distraction, and hadn't figured out exactly what business I would go into. It was like the angel on one shoulder and the devil on the other.

Although it's not in strict chronological order, the tug of war in my head played out like this:

Pull to the new: I started changing the way I spoke about myself. When people asked what I did, I would say, "I work as a graphic designer, but I want to run my own business." My whole language started to change, and I put my dream at the forefront. I spoke this new identity into being, in a way. This is who I am and I'm going to put that first and foremost. I tried this out for the first time at a good friend's birthday lunch. With as much confidence as I could muster, I said it to a couple I had just met and, to my delight, neither of them laughed in my face. It might sound silly, but that moment was hugely impactful to me. They took what I said at face value and believed me. It was a turning point. I was beginning to leave my old identity behind me and forge a new one that felt right to me.

Push to the old: I still had moments of extreme self-doubt. One minute I felt certain and the next minute, my previous failures would come back to haunt me and I'd question whether I was delusional even considering trying again. My self-belief was shaky to say the least. I wanted to trust what I had committed to but I still had a hard time believing it could be possible because of my past experiences.

> *Steve Jobs famously asked, "If this was the last day of your life, is this what you want to do?"*
>
> *And I'd be screaming inside, "No, no!" but I still had to go to work and get my job done.*

Pull: I started reading books about women in business to learn as much as I could about what it took to make a business successful and sustainable. Reading stories like the food from Martha Stewart's first catering gig melting in the sun helped me lighten up and realise that even the most well-known people in business had their fair share of mishaps. What had made them household names wasn't the fact they hadn't made any mistakes, it was their ability to bounce back from failures and keep moving forward towards their vision.

Push: I used shopping as a way to distract myself. We'd recently returned from a dream trip around Europe, where I had indulged in a spot of European shopping, and treated myself to a divine pair of expensive Christian Louboutin shoes from the flagship store in Paris – a longtime dream in itself. The famous red-soled shoes favoured by many celebrities are often outrageously styled with Lady Gaga-style spikes, sparkles and bright colours, and the ones I chose had all of those! But within a week of being back home, I went to the mall and bought a new pair of high-tops for the gym and a handbag. I used it as a quick pick-me-up to numb the pain of continuing to do something I knew I no longer wanted to do.

It was a worry that I was using spending as a quick fix. I had the disposable income and I justified it by saying it was a way of balancing out the unpleasant feelings I was going through at the time.

Pull: I signed up for Dr. Demartini's Master 'Planning for Life' course in Auckland in October 2013. I spent three days deepening my understanding of the concepts I'd been introduced to via his talks. Inspired by what I learned on the course around the power of taking control over your finances to enable greater choices in your life, I committed to curb my spending and started to save to pave the way for my business journey. I worked out that I needed to get financially prepared if I wanted to leave the stability of my job and go back into running a business. To help me do this, I set myself a small budget to spend each month on stationery. The pleasant side-effect was it made these purchases seem more special and the buzz I got from seeing my 'escape money' account grow replaced the need for a quick fix from shopping.

Push: Coming back to work after our trip, I got the sense that I wasn't missed and that even some of my workmates would rather I hadn't come back at all. I was in charge of managing the design jobs between myself and another designer, and one of my colleagues told me that things had felt so much more productive when they'd been able to brief my designer directly while I was away. Even though the insights I'd gained from learning about my values and strengths had helped me understand my role wasn't a match for me, I felt like I wasn't needed. That was hard to hear and my ego took a hit.

Pull: I went to see Irish band The Script in concert and, feeling uplifted by their song 'Hall of Fame', I wrote the words, 'Every day is one step closer to my dream job', on a whiteboard in our pantry. This visual reminder inspired me every time I reached for a snack or was in the kitchen.

Push: Even though I continued to read books about successful women in business, I still carried a belief that I couldn't possibly be capable of building businesses like these women had. Surely, I told myself, if it was meant to be it should come to me easily. I still felt so confused about what kind of business I would start and would constantly question whether it was even a good idea to go after this dream.

Pull: Even though I wasn't in business, I decided to sign-up to a women's business event and surround myself with inspiring women. Armed only with my Louboutins and an insatiable curiosity, I eavesdropped on the conversations between women I viewed as successful because I had seen them advertising and promoting their businesses around Auckland. Listening to them share real and honest stories of staffing challenges, marketing and pricing worries, helped me realise they all struggled at times too! I started to really embrace the belief that perfection wasn't a prerequisite for business success.

Push: Every Saturday, I'd go to my BODYJAM™ class. After sweating it out and dancing up a storm, my friend Kate – who I'd inspired to come to the classes with me – and I would often go for brunch afterwards and talk about life. We talked about everything. I remember saying to her during one of our chats, "Oh, I'll just get pregnant and have a baby and take maternity leave. That's when I'll figure out what business to start." There was a part of me that thought succeeding in having a baby and going on maternity leave would give me a ticket out of my 9 to 5 struggles.

Pull: With her wisdom, Kate replied, "Chances are you'll have a baby, and you'll have no time to figure out what you want to do." I love having conversations with this friend because she gently challenges me, in the kindest way possible. Damn it, I thought. She's right. I can't keep thinking I can get another job or have a baby to solve all my problems. Something was telling me I needed to figure it out before adding more complications to my life, no matter how impossible it seemed!

Push: Instead of solely focusing on starting a business, I started exploring different roles that I thought might be more suitable while I worked on my business aspirations. I put my CV forward for roles that were out of my comfort zone but more aligned with the strengths and values I had identified. I still wasn't 100% convinced I was cut out for the world of business.

Pull: Inspired by my sister's departure from the 9 to 5, I started looking into alternative ways of making money and read a book one weekend called Click Millionaires, which was about starting an online business.

Push: I felt super-inspired by the possibility of running an online business but my enthusiasm was crushed when I returned to work on Monday to find nothing had changed. I so desperately wanted things to change for the better and I felt frustrated by the reality that simply reading a book hadn't changed my situation overnight. I wanted to fast forward to the day when I was a successful entrepreneur like the people I had been reading about.

Pull: I remembered one of the Demartini techniques around finding gratitude in challenges that was designed to help you balance your moods so you could focus on your long-term vision and not get caught up in short-term frustrations about how you wished life should be. Each time I felt frustration arise I would do the exercise, sometimes it was daily.

I wrote lists of what I could be grateful for in my current situation and reflected on what could be the possible drawbacks of skipping over the time and effort required to build strong foundations in a business. I began to see how taking my time to get things established would mean I could stick at it long term. My frustration at being stuck in a 9 to 5 job eased ever so slightly.

Even though my desires extended beyond what I was doing, I could be grateful for the income I was earning that had allowed me to invest in developing myself. I started to look for opportunities in my current role to develop myself and find reasons to be proud of myself, even if I didn't want to stay there long-term. Instead of resisting everything, I started seeing a multitude of ways in which being where I was could ultimately serve my future dreams.

One of these was starting to take responsibility and following up on things people had asked me to do.

As 2013 drew to a close, I took some time to open my Happiness Jar. I felt inspired to not only read each piece of paper, but to categorise them. As I opened each bundled up piece of paper and relived the moments of joy, I put them into neat little piles of similar things, curious to see what had made me the most happy.

There were piles of obvious things: BODYJAM™ classes, trips to kikki.K, concerts, snuggles with my kitties, chats with my friends and husband. But there was also a pile that caught me by surprise.

It was a pile of moments where I had overcome challenges at work, particularly when dealing with difficult people or challenging situations. Interesting, I thought. I had historically avoided conflict, but there it was written multiple times on brightly coloured pieces of paper – overcoming challenges made me happy! Maybe I didn't need someone to buy me a new life after all?

This exercise and all the moments of self-discovery during my year of doing more of what made me happy made me realise that my life, although it wasn't 'perfect' was worth living. I didn't need a new life, I just needed to fall in love with the life I already had!

Ready to move through the messy middle?

You can pause here and go to **page 131** to complete the journaling exercises for this section.

Become a match for what you are seeking.

CHAPTER 4

Inner Grit

Building my conviction

I began 2014 more in love with my life, but I still felt stuck. I felt confident telling people outside of work about my aspirations to be in business but I didn't feel any closer to living that reality. As I went back to work after the summer break, I struggled to handle the discomfort and disconnect of living a life that I knew did not match my personality or strengths. It was like a straitjacket. I felt a sense of dread as I drove into the driveway - swiping through the gate felt like I was losing a bit of my soul in the process.

But it still didn't feel like the right time to make a move. Over the break, I was browsing the career section of the kikki.K website and saw an opening advertised to become their NZ Workshop Consultant. I thought it would be an ideal role for me as I had loved my workshop experience. But we were still trying for a baby so I thought that switching jobs now wouldn't be sensible because I'd risk forfeiting maternity pay. I was still afraid to trust myself. The sense of urgency was building, and an internal voice turning louder like a stage whisper was saying: You have to do something Michelle, you now have all this knowledge, all this great awareness, and you know this is not where you want to be or are meant to be.

I got out of my car to begin the walk up to the office. I was wearing a black dress and shoes with fluorescent yellow toe tips and black and white patterned heels to cheer myself up. This is known as dopamine dressing by the way, and it works! My shoes were a little small, but I bought them because I loved how they looked. As I tottered along, I said to myself with a sense of conviction, "This is my last year here. My last 'first day of the year' here."

As I settled into the working year, a thought occurred to me. I think my colleagues are relating to me as my role, not as Michelle, a person with hopes and dreams outside of these walls. Perhaps it was the summer break at the beach or my recent Dr. Demartini gratitude practice that gave me clarity, but it made sense. Of course, I hadn't shared my desires to move on with any of my workmates in case word got around and I was asked to leave. As far as they were concerned, the person in my role should perform the assigned duties to the best of their abilities.

I started to notice what was behind the tone they would use with me when I hadn't delivered. The behaviour I interpreted as 'nasty' from them was actually their frustration bubbling over. I couldn't blame them. If I was trying to get something done and someone wasn't delivering, I'd probably feel similar. It wasn't their fault I felt trapped in a role that no longer fit but I still didn't feel confident enough to leave.

While my attitude had improved, thanks to my gratitude practice, and I could do my job, it took so much effort to make myself do it. After doing all the strengths and values work, I discovered that although I was competent at designing, it drained my energy. I would finish a piece of work and instead of feeling proud, I felt empty. The joy had gone for me.

I liked the meetings I got to be part of as part of my team leader role – talking to people and strategising on projects energised me. But when I had to spend hours sitting quietly behind a computer finishing a design or routine tasks, it reminded me of forcing my cat Charlie into a cage to go to the vet. The sight of the cat carrier sent him running. I felt like running some days.

But I had to do it because part of my role was design and that was what I was paid to do. Every time I sat down to concentrate, I wanted to get up and walk away and chat with someone in the coffee room. I'd lost my desire to learn anything new about design or to climb the ladder in that career.

Returning from one of my 'coffee breaks', I noticed how I found talking to people in the staff kitchen energising. I loved asking them about their aspirations and interests. I felt present and uplifted after those kinds of conversations. I thought: Wouldn't it be fun to be paid to talk? I thought it sounded impossible, but it seemed like a marvellous idea!

It was enough to remind me of my quest to figure out what I was put on this earth to do and continue towards my dream of running my own business.

Songs started to play on the radio during my morning commute that felt like they were being sung directly to me. Katy Perry's 'Roar' and Rudimental's 'Not Giving In' were like battle-cries that I could sing to keep me focused on my end goal.

Scan to listen to the song or visit
michellekeating.com/shinemusic

Becoming a B-School butterfly

Another light appeared at the end of the tunnel when my sister sent me a link to a website with a note: "I think you might like this, Michelle."

It was a link to a video series promoting Marie Forleo's B-School.

As I watched the first video, I instantly fell in love with Marie, an entrepreneur from New Jersey. She has her own YouTube channel where she talks about business. I related to her because she also loved pretty things, is feminine and she'd walked a similar path of not knowing who she wanted to be and had ended up running a wildly successful online business.

Once a year, Marie opens enrolments to her eight-week course B-School, which is focused on all the mechanics of building your own online business. Enrolments were open for this year's intake and while the course price felt like a huge investment, I was frustrated by my own progress – I was still stuck in the nightmare of my 9 to 5, not knowing how to achieve my business dreams. Perhaps, I thought, B-School has come along at the right time to give me a push in the right direction.

I binge-watched all of Marie's free YouTube videos, trying to make a decision about whether or not to join. She would end every video by saying, "Keep going for your dreams because the world needs that special something only you have". I needed to hear that. I talked it through with my sister. I thought if I wanted to have a ten-million-dollar business (an idea I had imagined in one of my morning meditations) then I needed to invest in myself to get there. It was scary but it also felt like everything that I wanted and needed.

Still, deciding whether to drop a few thousand dollars on my dream was a big decision. My husband's work contract had recently ended, so I was temporarily the sole income earner for our family. In the days leading up to the course registration cut-off, I spent hours looking at the website, reading the stories of other people who had already completed the course and felt inspired by how many were living their business dreams.

In the end, I decided my dreams were worth the investment and, with my husband's blessing, I paid for B-School on my credit card. I trusted that what I would learn in the course would allow me to repay the cost of the course, as well as help me move towards the life I wanted to be living. It was a leap of faith, but it felt right to be taking it.

After I signed up, I posted a quote on my Facebook profile that summed up my commitment:

> *"How does one become a butterfly? You have to want to learn to fly so much that you are willing to give up being a caterpillar."* – TRINA PAULUS

I was ready to give up being a caterpillar!

The decision to join B-School, it seemed, would change the course of my life. There was something about making that level of investment in myself that meant I had to up my game. I felt I had no choice but to take it seriously.

The course had eight modules with a mixture of video and audio. I'd listen in the car on my way to work. Marie is talented. She doesn't sugar-coat business – she tells it how it is. In one of the first videos she said, "If your business is not making money, you don't have a business." I was ready to hear it. I needed to hear the truth of what I was getting myself into, but Marie did it in such a skilful way it didn't scare me off. I got excited. Really excited.

The course came with access to an inspiring Facebook community filled with other people who felt just like I did – stuck in their 9 to 5 jobs but wanting so much more for their lives. Plus, it had other business owners who were way ahead of me, living proof that it is possible to do what you love and make a great living.

During my lunch breaks, I would spend time in the Facebook group interacting with others. I felt like I had found my tribe, somewhere I belonged. I wasn't crazy or alone for wanting more for my life.

Buoyed by this confidence, I decided it was time to get serious. I needed to commit to a date to hand in my resignation.

The beginning of the end

At the start of the year, I had bought a blue 2014 kikki.K diary with 'Best Year Yet' on the cover. I loved that diary. It was part of kikki.K's collection around the theme of Follow Your Path and as soon as I saw the window display, I felt like it was talking directly to me. It felt fitting to be committing fully to following my own path and forging a new direction for myself.

The Best Year Yet diary had blank spaces and all these inspiring quotes. I used to sit outside in the mornings and create some calm with yoga and meditation and then write in my journal. These rituals helped to centre me so I could better face a day in the office.

On a slightly chilly morning in late March, I wrote my leaving date and committed to it. That date was 31 August 2014.

I chose 31 August because it felt far enough away for me to complete B-School and set up a solid plan for my business but close enough that it would help me manage my frustrations about work as I had something to look forward to – the end of August was my target.

The act of writing down the date and committing to it was the mind shift I needed. I felt bulletproof as I walked into the office that day. A smile of satisfaction on my face as I felt confident that I finally had a ticket out of my situation once and for all.

I'd already set up monthly savings to grow my 'escape money' fund, so I doubled down on working through B-School to get clear on which direction I was going to take in business. One of the resources in B-School was called 'Start the Right Business'. It was a structured way of evaluating my multitude of ideas to find a direction I could take that had the greatest chance of success.

> *It was just what I needed. As someone who is a little prone to having an idea and running with it, this module allowed me to look closely at my ideas and figure out whether they would make a viable business (or not). I started to gain real traction.*

I spent my Saturday afternoons after BODYJAM™ working on my business dream. Initially I had an idea of creating beautiful dessert tables to combine my love of beautiful things and baking. Following Marie's advice, I Googled local people already doing it as a business so I could learn from their experiences. I felt so excited, having written a lengthy email to request a conversation about the reality of the type of business I was considering. I felt another rush of excitement when I got my first reply! I had a different approach to follow and I felt like I was making real progress.

Before I booked a time to speak to the person who had replied to me, I gave myself a quick reality check and realised that it was highly likely that type of business would end up being the same low margin/high time commitment model as Cupcake Love. I congratulated myself for doing the exploration first and recognising that it wasn't a path I should go down. My love of baking and decorating could remain a beloved hobby while I explored more sustainable business opportunities.

Instead of seeing it as a failure, I kept going. I looked at idea after idea in search of my ideal business. I thought about starting a blog called Live Like It's Your Birthday in honour of my love of celebrating and how I had found happiness in my everyday life. With my sister's coaching help, I wrote the first draft of an eBook to share my thoughts on how to make every day feel like a celebration. I went so far as to design a logo and set up a Wordpress website.

But, when it came time to write my first blog for the website I couldn't think of anything positive to write, I felt like I wasn't exactly practising what I was preaching. You see, not only was I dealing with a job I wasn't happy in, but our plan to conceive also wasn't happening. We tried to get pregnant. We really tried. But it wasn't happening for us. We ended up needing to seek fertility support. That had added another layer of stress to 2014 and it felt inauthentic to pretend everything was rosy and happy.

After the highs of the previous year, 2014 was beginning to feel like the perfect shitstorm. Excuse the language but I don't think there's a polite way of putting it.

My determination to figure out my path kept me going. After enduring a particularly invasive test that our fertility specialist recommended, I came up with the idea of creating a business helping people get organised. A diagnosis of ADD in late 2012 had led me on a journey to becoming more organised, so I thought combining my knowledge and personal experience with my love of pretty stationery and organising products was an option worth exploring.

This time I actually followed through with Marie's suggestion to talk to 10 people already running a professional organising business – a whole industry I hadn't even known existed before I started researching. Having learnt from my previous attempt, instead of a long winded email, I created a short, sharp email and sent it to some of the organisers I found via the B-School website and a directory I'd discovered of organisers in Australia and New Zealand.

Over the next couple of weeks, I snuck out on my lunch break to the carpark to make phone calls. It felt exhilarating! I had hope and a purpose to balance out what was happening in the office.

Change for good

This renewed sense of energy and purpose, combined with having a planned leaving date and a greater awareness that I may have been contributing to the undesired behaviour of my colleagues gave me the courage to do something I had been avoiding – address the tension between myself and my designer.

I felt like I had nothing to lose.

Along with the tensions that had arisen between myself and members of the wider marketing team, things had become increasingly toxic with my direct report. Our interactions were strained and I felt an air of disapproval whenever I approached her.

We were polar opposites, looks and personality wise. I wore high heels and dresses to work, she wore sneakers, t-shirts and shorts. Where I had a pop-princess vibe, she had a rock-chick air about her. I liked to chat, she liked to get things done. My bright and bubbly personality was in direct contrast to her more straight-shooting, no-nonsense way of relating to people.

When we started working together, we were both graphic designers within the marketing team and we had been close. In more recent years, she had been seconded to a project which meant I was mostly managing contractors, so we hadn't had as much to do with each other work-wise, but we knew each other well.

When her project came to an end and she resumed her usual duties within the team, I noticed a change in our dynamic. Instead of being jovial together like we once were, our interactions were strained. Instead of binding together over problems, it felt like a battleground between us. Her tone towards me became increasingly short and snappy and I couldn't understand why. Because of the internal struggles I had going on, I initially avoided conversations as much as possible but it only seemed to make things worse.

It became unbearable for me. As well as feeling heavy with my own frustration and confusion, here I was in a situation where every day felt like I was waiting for the next verbal attack. I would go home either in tears or enraged. I leaned on my manager Kimberley, my husband, and anyone who would listen, exclaiming how unfair her behaviour was. I would spend hours ruminating over it, wishing it was different. Why did she have to be so negative towards me? Why couldn't she be positive about things? Couldn't she see how hurtful and upsetting her behaviour was?

An opportunity arose for me to tackle the issue head on. We had staff performance reviews coming up and the company had changed the way they were doing them to try and shift the culture – to improve communication and cohesion within teams.

The interactions between us had been noticed by the wider team and it wasn't just me who had been on the receiving end of her sometimes harsh tone. It was up to me to address it. The thought of confronting her behaviour was terrifying; I really didn't want to go there. It would have been easier to just leave and not deal with it, let it be someone else's problem.

I had an opinion about her. I viewed her tone and manner as a sign that she was unhappy with me on some level and felt like she was taking it out on me. I wanted her to be happy and light like my personality, and cursed her for constantly raining on my happiness parade.

When I prepared the documents for her performance review, I started off by making a list of all the negative things I had experienced – her abrasive tone, slamming things loudly on the desk, and generally negative attitude towards other people in the office. I was in fight mode. I wanted to release all my pent-up frustration and spew at her, "You did this, this and this, and you need to change!"

I looked at the list I'd written on the page. While it felt incredibly cathartic to get it all out, something about seeing it all written down made me pause. They were all points about how her behaviour made me feel. The concept of balance that I'd learnt from Dr. Demartini flashed into my mind. I remember him saying, if you want a one-sided life, if you want everything to be nice all the time, then you're going to attract negativity to balance that out because life has two sides. And when we can embrace both sides – the good and the bad, the pleasure and the pain – then we are coming from a centred place. When we lean too heavily towards one side, we'll inevitably attract people and external situations to try and wake us up and restore that balance.

I sat for a moment, stunned at my realisation. I picked up my pen and started to balance out my initial list with a list of the good things she brought to her role. She gets her work done on time, she's never late to work, and she cares deeply about the accuracy of what we produce.

Suddenly, I saw it. Her behaviour only flared up as a direct result of me avoiding what I should be doing as a manager. It was my job to have the tough conversations and address problems head-on. But I was doing the opposite. I was avoiding the tough conversations; I'd try to laugh off and ignore the difficult things and then complain to others about her behaviour. But it was my avoidance that would spark the behaviour in her. It was like a feedback mechanism, and it wasn't until I sat back and looked at it that I noticed she was doing me a favour by helping me see what I'd been avoiding. When I took a more balanced view, I could see how my avoidance had contributed to the situation. It was the wakeup call I needed.

Because I hadn't wanted to address it, I could see that subconsciously I was putting up with the undesirable aspects of her behaviour because I needed her and I didn't want to do all the design work. If she wasn't there, I'd have to do it, and I didn't want to do it!

I thought of the theatre show, Wicked, that I'd seen with a friend. In it there's the good witch who dresses like a fairy princess, representing everything nice – that reminded me of myself. And then there's the bad witch, dressed in black who is negatively perceived by everyone – that's how I saw her. But (spoiler alert) you find out that it's actually the good witch who is the 'bad' one but, because the 'good' witch has a nicer demeanour, she gets away with it. I played the song 'For Good' from the soundtrack in my car while driving home and felt a deep sense of gratitude. What I'd seen from our challenging dynamic was changing me for good.

Scan to listen to the song or visit
michellekeating.com/shinemusic

It still felt so nerve-wracking getting ready to share my thoughts in our review. I had never delivered this kind of feedback before and I was worried how she might receive it. I imagined the possibility of her punching me in the face and storming out. I leaned on Kimberley for support and she sent me the song 'Brave' by Sara Bareilles. I shared my concerns and plan with the HR Manager and the consultant who was helping roll out the changes to the staff performance reviews. Their support and encouragement made me feel brave.

**Scan to listen to the song or visit
michellekeating.com/shinemusic**

When I went into the review meeting, I was shaking and felt physically sick. I tried my hardest to stay calm as I delivered both sides of the feedback I'd prepared. The meeting ended somewhat awkwardly but thankfully she didn't punch me in the face.

To my surprise, the next day when we met up for our usual weekly update meeting, she said, "Thank you, Michelle." She'd shown the report to her partner, and he'd said, "Yep, you can be like that sometimes." The exercise had been revealing for her as well. We were both being changed for good.

Dressed for Success?

The deadline for handing in my resignation was edging closer. I was still in the process of working through Marie's 'Start the Right Business' when Angela, a friend who always generously listened to me as I complained about my circumstances and grappled with what to do, sent me an email with the words "Now could THIS be you my darling?", followed by the job description for a part-time job she had seen advertised at a charity she volunteered at called Dress for Success. It was an Office Manager role which played to my strengths, particularly in the area of systems and organisation. It was also highly people-focused and I'd be supporting a women-focused organisation that aligned with my values. Plus, there was no graphic design involved.

This could be my ticket out. It was only 32.5 hours a week which would mean I'd still have some income coming in but I'd have more time to work on starting a business and I'd be doing something I enjoy. Not to mention the timing was perfectly aligned with my planned date to hand in my resignation. It felt like it was all working out. I enthusiastically applied.

I was sitting outside in the sun in my usual lunchtime spot down the side of the office building when I saw a notification that Lani, the Executive Director of Dress for Success had viewed my LinkedIn profile. A flutter of excitement rose up in my stomach. Perhaps this meant I might get an interview!

Sure enough, I was offered an interview time – scheduled for a week before the leaving date I'd committed to in my diary. I booked a leave day from work and felt certain that this was a sign that things were heading in the right direction. Ironically, I also booked a meeting with a recruiter for graphic design roles following the interview. I still wasn't quite ready to fully trust my new direction.

With 31 August fast approaching and the Dress for Success interview locked in, I typed up my resignation letter. I thought that everything was neat – I'd addressed the issues with my workmate, I had saved up quite a bit of money to start my business, and I'd been working my way through B-School. And now this. The stars were aligning.

The day of the interview came and nervously I made my way via the motorway to the Dress for Success offices. I wore the same black dress and fluorescent yellow tipped shoes I had worn on the first day of the working year to boost my confidence. Only this time it was the middle of winter so I had sheer tights on to keep warm. I wasn't 100% in love with the winter version of the outfit but I felt like it presented a professional but funky look and I wouldn't freeze when I got out of the car.

I shared how the role aligned with my strengths and I listened enthusiastically to Lani explain more. She gave me a tour of the showroom where they helped women get ready for interviews and new jobs by providing clothing, accessories, and styling support. I left hoping I'd made a good impression at the interview and began imagining what it might be like to work alongside Lani and contribute to their work.

I sat in the car for a few minutes afterwards before I headed into my next meeting. Was this the right move for me? I questioned myself. Yes, it aligns with my strengths of strategically building systems, love of organisation and ticked the box for my top WOO strength of meeting and greeting a variety of people. I'd done everything I could, put my best high-heeled foot forward and now it was time to wait to hear whether I'd be offered the role. I had so much at stake with my resignation letter typed up and ready to go, surely this was going to come through so I could make all my dreams come true.

I waited in anticipation to hear back. On Saturday, five days after the interview, as I was sitting up in bed, about to get ready for my BODYJAM™ class, I checked my inbox and saw I had received an email from Lani. Butterflies filled my stomach as I opened it. I quickly scanned the words looking for the news I so badly wanted to hear.

My heart sank as I read the words I didn't want to see. She thanked me for my time, but regretfully advised that I had been unsuccessful. They had chosen someone else more suitable for the role. The second half of the sentence hit me like a truck. This wasn't what I expected or wanted. The room felt like it was starting to spin as I re-read her words in disbelief. A mix of anger and despair started to rise within me. This was not how this was supposed to go, this was my ticket out of my job. What the heck am I going to do now?, I anguished.

The disappointment hit me hard. I thought I had done everything I needed to do. I set myself a resignation date, I'd saved money, I'd found something that felt aligned with my strengths and values. What was I going to tell everyone who knew about my intention to resign from my job? Was I seriously destined to be a failure at this too?

I felt sick. As tears began to well up in my eyes, I felt my familiar instinct arise to shut down the feelings of despair and upset that were rising in me. The instinct to brush it off and pretend everything was okay was right there. Except this time it felt too big to contain. This felt huge for me. I wanted that job, I wanted to hand in my resignation.

I let the tears flow. I didn't brush them away, laugh it off, or plaster a smile on. I allowed myself to feel the disappointment. I had set myself a massive goal, I went for it and I'd fallen short. It hurt.

After a few minutes, an unfamiliar sense of calm washed over me. As I sat in the stillness, I felt a sense of certainty come over me, similar to how I felt after reading about Walt Disney and deciding I definitely wanted to be in business. A kind, wise whisper came into my mind, it said: What if you weren't supposed to get that job? What if you are destined to be in business? What if this is a good thing?

I sat with those words. What if this was a good thing? I felt a fire of determination begin to rise in me and the sudden urge to pick up my phone to search for some inspiration. I came across a quote with a graphic of an ocean liner on the water. It said, 'If your ship doesn't come in, swim out to it'. Even though I didn't get the role, something told me this wasn't the end.

Ready to access your inner grit?

You can pause here and go to **page 149** to complete the journaling exercises for this section.

Giant leaps are actually a whole lot of baby steps strung together.

CHAPTER 5
A leap of faith

The problem is me

I still had my resignation day of 31 August in my diary, but I didn't hand in my resignation letter. It didn't feel like the right thing to do. After the Dress for Success experience, I felt like I should sit tight and save more money first and have a clearer plan if I was going to stick to my goal of being in business.

But the resignation letter wasn't wasted. I still had it saved. It was a case of when I leave my job, not if.

It was difficult letting 31 August pass by, still in my job. While it had been my choice to stay, it felt painful not having a definite end in sight. Despite my initial surge of determination, in the weeks that followed, I began to feel more confused than ever. We were still trying to conceive without success. We had begun seeing a naturopath who had advised me to follow a strict diet, which only added to my mental stress. I wasn't able to cheer myself up with sweet treats in the same way I normally would and felt resentful that I had to go to such extreme lengths to fall pregnant.

In the aftermath of my attempted resignation, it dawned on me that I thought that one of the main reasons I hated my job so much was because of my issues with my workmates.

But in the weeks that had followed the performance review, the working relationship with my designer had dramatically improved. Part of my review suggested that she do the CliftonStrengths® Assessment and we discovered that while we were very different personality-wise, we each had strengths that complemented each other. Where I had strength with people, she had strength in consistency, so it made sense that we each take the lead in these areas. We also uncovered that we had overlapping strengths in strategic thinking, which meant when we worked through certain problems together the quality and speed of the results were multiplied. Understanding and accepting each other reduced the tension dramatically. It was huge.

That major problem was solved. So why was I still feeling so out of sorts?

I had to sit in this space of ownership. It's actually me. It's not anyone else's fault. I can't blame anyone else for not wanting to be here. There's no scapegoat here.

As usual, the perfect song came along to confirm my thinking. As I listened to 'It's Not Right for You' by The Script, I let the message sink in. I needed to acknowledge my feelings. Continuing to be a graphic designer was not right for me.

Scan to listen to the song or visit
michellekeating.com/shinemusic

The company had been so supportive through the review process, yet I still didn't want to be there. I had to really sit with the problem and the uncomfortable truth: Maybe I was the problem.

It came to me as I was walking through the factory area one morning. There was nothing wrong with the job, it was me. In the end it came down to this – the products they made and the industry they were in just didn't light me up. I craved different things in my life.

It was time to get off this mountain.

Afraid to stay put, but terrified to move on

With the problem with my colleague no longer hanging over me, I thought my path would have been clear. I couldn't understand why in my heart I knew what I wanted to be doing, yet I found myself still unable to move forward confidently. What was wrong with me? Why couldn't I figure this out?

Thankfully, the answer came to me via one of my B-School buddies, Jen Stemp.

I had resonated with her posts in the B-School Facebook community and subscribed to her Freedom Leap newsletter.

One morning, I spotted an email in my inbox with the subject line: Scared to stay put, but terrified to move forwards? Do this. I eagerly opened the email to find out more.

The email had an exercise inviting me to look at the different scenarios I was considering and the pros and cons of each to try and uncover what was really keeping me stuck.

I knew I needed to do something, so I grabbed my notebook and created columns with the headings:

Stay put.	Get another job.	Start a business.

When I started writing all the pros of starting my own business, I noticed that it all stacked up. Words like self-expression and freedom jumped off the page. I could see it all clearly, why wasn't I living it already?

When I looked at getting another job, it was clear that it wouldn't address my longing to do something different. Sure, it would improve things for a little while, but the feeling of wanting to know what my reciprocal joy is would remain.

Then I looked at the pros I had written of staying where I was and not doing anything. The status quo had some pros: Security, safety, a reliable pay cheque.

Even though I felt certain about my desire to be in business, the sense of safety and security I was getting from the job was keeping me stuck. That was it! I knew what I wanted but I didn't fully believe in myself yet. I was afraid to let go of the safety net.

A lightbulb went on inside my head, that was it! No matter how much I wanted to be in business, I needed to let go of the safety and security of a consistent pay cheque. I needed to get comfortable with feeling uncomfortable. If I'm going to embark on this entrepreneurial journey, I'm going to need to be okay with the unknown because there are no guarantees in business.

No matter how much I saved or how much research I did, I realised that if I didn't embrace the unknown that comes with moving away from the 9 to 5, I would forever keep waiting for the perfect time to make a leap.

It helped me make sense of why I was saying one thing (I want to be in business), but doing another (staying in my job). It gave me a clue as to what was really holding me back, something that would lead me to one of the greatest realisations along my journey.

Shortly after doing this exercise, I had a meeting with one of my colleagues for a design briefing. It was for a project that deep down I knew I didn't want to do but had to as part of my role. My colleague was really excited but I was thinking, I'd rather chew my arm off than do this.

I did my best to act enthusiastic but afterwards I felt like I was going to explode with frustration. I sat down at my desk and, staring at my computer screen, I internally screamed "I don't want to do this because I don't want to do this!"

Wow! The realisation finally dawned on me. There really was no other reason than I didn't want to do it. It wasn't because I had a mortgage to pay or any other external reasoning I had been thinking. It really was because I knew in my heart that this wasn't what I was meant to be doing.

I was starting to listen to myself once and for all.

Bali to the rescue

All of my emotions came to a head after a routine appointment with our naturopath to assess our progress. I updated him with what was going on, trying to hold it together as best I could. The truth was, I resented having to be there at all. Why did we have to go to all this trouble when getting pregnant seemingly happened so easily for others? Everywhere I looked I saw pregnant women or 'Baby On Board' signs on the back of cars. I wondered if it would ever happen for us. It was absolute torture at times.

When I mentioned my period was a few days late, he mentioned something I didn't understand about HCG levels and getting a blood test, but he didn't think I was pregnant. Great, not only was I a wreck but also not pregnant – again. I got the blood test done before heading back to work and waited days for an answer, feeling like I was a bit all over the place. A few days later, I went over to a friend's house and burst into tears over a simple comment someone made about having a family. It was so embarrassing. What was going on with me?

Our naturopath called to say there was a slight rise in my HCG levels so I should have another blood test, but he still didn't think I was pregnant. I felt so stressed having to have yet another test.

My parents could obviously sense my distress with both our fertility struggles and my work woes. Out of the blue, they offered to pay for a trip to Bali so I could visit my sister. She and her partner had decided to move there after she'd completed her life coaching certification in Canada. I was thrilled – I would get a break from all the stresses of work and the disappointment of failing to conceive. I could simply forget about all of it and enjoy some downtime in a serene environment with my sister who had been so supportive during this time.

It didn't take me long to organise my flights to Bali and organise leave from work. It gave me a renewed sense of purpose and something exciting to look forward to. Then finally, after almost a week, the specialist called me to say: "Congratulations, you're pregnant."

But I had already started bleeding the day before. I was miscarrying.

After over a year of trying to conceive, I was finally pregnant and didn't know, and now I know I'm no longer pregnant. I had a hard time getting my head around the whole thing. I was angry with the naturopath, why didn't he take better care of me? He'd left me in a state of unknown for over a week. Would things have been different if he had got back to me straight away? It explained why I had felt so strongly when I was sitting at my computer – it was the hormones of early pregnancy.

I don't know what I would've done if my parents hadn't given me that trip to Bali. I really believe it would have broken me. As it was, I had to go through the medical formalities of a miscarriage just days before I flew out. I was barely holding it together.

I made it to Bali. And, thank goodness, because I was a wreck. I was so grateful to be with my sister and her partner at the time. There was something about being there, a magical kind of energy.

Embracing Grace

After an initial tearful greeting as I expressed all of the pain and confusion of our miscarriage, I was slowly able to put down the weight of everything I'd been carrying. Anna and her partner Dan introduced me to Bali life. Whizzing through the noisy, busy streets on the back of Anna's scooter, dining at beautiful beach clubs at sunset and visiting quaint yoga studios was a world away from the stresses and strains of home. I was so grateful to have time to process everything away from my job and the office.

Sitting in the blissfully warm sunshine by the pool at their villa, I took some time to read ***Daily Love: Growing into Grace,*** a newly released book by Mastin Kipp. I'd come across Mastin through B-School and pre-ordered a copy before I left for Bali. Still wrestling with what I wanted and needed to do next, reading his book was like a soothing balm.

Mastin shares his story of hitting rock-bottom, living in the tiny pool house of his ex-girlfriend's parents. When he began listening to the small voice within and trusting the invisible force surrounding us all, who he referred to as the Divine/God, he courageously took steps into the unknown. This led to him building the Daily Love platform, appearing on Oprah's Super Soul 100, and impacting over half a million people with his inspiration.

Until then, my experience of anything to do with God had been through Sunday School sessions as a child or feeling bored in mass as a teenager while attending a Catholic girl's high school. Reading Mastin's account of developing a faith in what he couldn't see and following the small, quiet nudges made me think of my recent experience after not getting the Dress for Success role.

Maybe those experiences were my own inner wisdom nudging me. Maybe this was the message I needed to hear most. To let go of what my head was trying to get me to do because it's the 'safe' thing to do and put my trust in a divine force outside of me. It was the perfect antidote to my recent realisation that I was staying in my job purely for the supposed safety and security.

I had savings in the bank, my inner wisdom had been screaming at me to leave my job but I'd been too afraid to take the leap. I decided that when I returned home from Bali, I was going to quit. Even though I wasn't entirely sure of how things would work out, I knew with absolute certainty I didn't want to continue in my current job.

After a few more days enjoying Bali life, including lots of yoga, swimming and good food, I came across a quote on a card in the local supermarket: "If you don't go after what you want, you'll never have it. If you don't ask, the answer is always no. If you don't step forward you're always in the same place." That was it! I had been holding on so tightly to what I didn't want, that there was no room for what I did want to show up.

> *I couldn't procrastinate any longer – now was the time to take that leap of faith. Trust the universe. Follow my inner wisdom and see where it takes me.*

With those words ringing in my ears and Mastin's story filling my heart, I decided to take an evening swim in the pool after my sister and her partner had gone to bed. Although it was late, the night was balmy and as I waded in the cool water, I noticed how water has a magical way of holding us. It felt like a beautiful metaphor for what I had been reading that day. It may sound strange, but it felt like a practice run for what I was about to do in real life.

When I walked in the water, I imagined what it would be like when I took a step in real life. I would be supported. Except in real life it wouldn't be by water, but by a supportive invisible force that I couldn't see, but needed to trust when I took steps towards what my heart desired. Towards what those whispers kept trying to tell me: You are meant for more, Michelle.

I needed to trust that I wasn't alone, that I would be guided to the next best thing for me. I didn't need to fully control the outcome. I had done the inner work necessary and saved enough resources to support myself as I ventured back into the world of business. I was ready to start climbing my mountain, but first I needed to let go of the one I was on.

Mastin's book and that experience in the pool sealed the deal for me. It was time for me to start trusting myself, my path, and the Divine. After I dried off and got ready for bed, I decided to check my email one last time, only to discover the first message in my inbox was Mastin's newsletter containing his latest video blog. I decided to have a quick watch, after all I had just had the most magical day reading and absorbing his book.

To my surprise, he had recorded the video in Ubud, the very place I had been just a few days before doing yoga. How cool was that? Mastin and I were in Bali at the same time. I remembered looking at his retreat earlier in the year but had no idea that the dates would coincide with my unexpected trip. I saw the video had a place to share comments so I typed up my heartfelt gratitude for everything I was taking away from his book. A few moments later I heard a ping, another email had come through – Mastin had replied to my comment straight away!

> *"Soooooo proud of you Michelle!!!*
> *KEEP GOING – KEEP TRUSTING! Waving from Ubud."*

A grin spread across my face and I hugged my phone close to my chest. This was a magical confirmation that I was doing the right thing. It was time to turn up the volume on the whispers of my soul and let them lead the way.

Faith

Fear

Taking the leap

Once I returned home, I didn't waste any time. I didn't want to lose any of the lessons and momentum from my transformative time in Bali.

I went out with my husband, Rob, for breakfast and told him I was going to hand in my notice at work. This was the right time for me to take a giant leap towards what I really wanted. He was really supportive, even though I'm sure he felt a little nervous for both of us.

I could finally open up to my colleagues about what I'd been through and what was happening for me. This was a giant leap in letting go of the life I didn't want and embracing the one I was imagining.

I shook like a leaf as I prepared to share the news with Kimberley. She was surprised, but understood. We had been close during my trials with my colleagues so I could sense her relief that I was doing something that felt right for me. She asked me when my leaving date would be and it dawned on me that I hadn't thought that far ahead. I had focused so much on gathering up the courage to hand in my resignation that I hadn't even considered when I would actually leave, LOL! She suggested I think about it overnight and let her know in the morning.

I left the meeting room like I was walking on air. I had done it. I was on my way. I didn't know the final destination, yet, but I knew I was headed in the right direction. As I sat down at my desk, taking it all in, I overheard Kimberley on the phone to the company's recruitment agency, letting them know we would need to hire a replacement for me. My chest tightened. Panic started to rise through my body. What had I done? I couldn't take it back now. Was I really doing the right thing?

Relax. I told myself. It's okay to feel afraid. Remember Mastin and the moment in the pool. Keep taking one step forward. It will be okay. I felt myself breathe out and my shoulders relaxed a little. I needed to keep remembering to trust that if I followed the whispers and nudges, it was going to be okay.

That night, I found the resignation letter that I had previously written and changed the date. I decided to give eight weeks' notice. I worked out that if

I left in February it was a time of the year when I knew companies would be recruiting, just in case I needed to get some kind of job. I was clearly still getting used to the idea that I could trust my decisions.

But, more significantly, I deliberately made my last day in the office line up with the upcoming Foo Fighters concert that I had tickets to. What better way to celebrate my steps towards doing what I was put on this earth to do than rocking out with one of my heroes and a shining example of someone doing exactly that.

Now that the initial doubt had worn away, I felt invincible. I knew, with a deep conviction, that I was choosing to be true to myself. By giving up my comfortable job, I was voting for my future self. It was absolutely the right thing to do.

I wanted a reminder of how this felt. So that weekend, after I handed in my resignation, I got a tattoo of a small diamond on my left wrist to remind me of my strength and hard-won, new-found sense of self. I remembered seeing a mural on the wall of the gym that said, 'Pressure Makes Diamonds.' It felt like the perfect symbol to capture my journey to this moment. A permanent reminder of what it meant to follow my inner compass, my sparkle, and not some kind of societal obligation.

As we drove home from the tattoo parlour Rihanna's 'Diamonds' song played on the radio. I couldn't help but smile.

Scan to listen to the song or visit michellekeating.com/shinemusic

With a wide open space of possibility ahead of me, I started making progress with creating a professional organising business, since this was the direction I'd landed on during my B-School exercises. I was going to call it Organised In Style. Ironically, all the research and learning how to set up a website from my previous Live Like It's Your Birthday idea was not wasted. No, it meant setting up the Organised In Style website was much more straightforward. The dots were beginning to join!

The Christmas holidays were bliss. I knew I wouldn't have to return to work dreading another year of being in a job I no longer wanted to do. I knew that if I kept moving in the right direction for me, things would have a way of working themselves out.

I was getting accustomed to listening to my intuition. So one morning during a long weekend in January when I had a sudden urge to have a look at the kikki.K website while making breakfast, I didn't hesitate to follow it.

I felt called to look at the Careers section. When I saw that there was a vacancy for the NZ Workshop Consultant, I had to look twice. My eyes blinked as I saw it clear as day. There it was again. The same position I had seen advertised the previous year was back. What the heck was this trying to tell me?

I'd made progress on starting my own organising business so wondered whether I should apply. As I read the position description more closely, it detailed that not only would I be presenting their in-store workshops but there was also the opportunity to help people organise their offices and homes. I could hardly believe it, here was the opportunity to get paid to talk AND help people get organised. It felt like a dream come true for me. I decided to trust my intuition and apply for the role and see what happened.

That night, I found my kikki.K journal from months earlier, where I had drafted a cover letter for the previously advertised role (but never managed to actually apply for it). I typed it up, adding a few new points before sending off my application. I sure as hell wasn't going to miss the opportunity this time.

A couple of days later, I was sitting on the couch after work when an email landed in my Inbox that would kickstart my new life. It was from kikki.K. "We'd love to interview you," it said. I danced around the room – I was that happy. One of my favourite brands ever. The company whose founder had re-inspired me to chase my dreams and helped me discover my own version of happiness now wanted to interview me? This time I wasn't on Cloud Nine, I was up in the stars, which felt like they were aligning in the most magical of ways.

On the first phone call to kikki.K, I spoke to the current Workshop Consultant, Isabelle. I took the call in a meeting room at work and nearly fell off my chair when one of the first things she said was, "I have to tell you something. It's likely to put you off. But you will need to run this as your own business."

Pinch me, I thought, is this actually happening? Working with kikki.K and they want me to run it like it's my own business! I replied as calmly as I could, trying my best to contain my delight at what was happening, "That wouldn't be a problem for me." What a dream – everything seemed to be falling into place. I had dreamed of running my own business, but not something quite as magical as this!

As the days at my job counted down, my interviews with kikki.K continued. I met with Isabelle and the NZ Regional Manager in person the next week, excitedly sharing both my personal kikki.K story and my passion for the workshops and products. Then I spoke to the workshop head in Australia. They all picked up on my passion for kikki.K and loved my story of my happiness journey and how following my intuition had led me to the role.

At the final stage of the interview process, I was asked to do a mock workshop presentation. As I was preparing, I couldn't help but smile as I realised that my time as a fairy princess had given me the presentation skills I needed for this kind of role. How else could a graphic designer end up facilitating workshops? It was another beautiful example of the dots of my life starting to line up.

I felt a real connection to the company, the team and the role, but I couldn't help feeling like I was somehow deserting Organised In Style if I was offered and accepted the role with kikki.K. Wasn't it my dream to run my own business, not work for someone else? After all, there was part of me that wanted to be like Kristina, not work for her company.

I thought back to everything I learned through B-School. Marie shared how it takes 18 months to 2 years to really establish a new business, and that during that time the majority of your time and energy would need to be dedicated to it. I thought about our dream to start a family. Maybe kikki.K was everything I needed right now. I would get to have the experience of running my own business while also being supported by a team and having the unique opportunity to learn about the inside workings of a business I admired. It felt like the biggest gift.

I decided that if I was offered the kikki.K role, I would accept it. I wouldn't be giving up on my business dreams.

I was choosing a path that supported our dreams of starting a family while also fulfilling my dream of doing what I loved.

On my last day of work, I wore my Louboutins from Paris and a brightly coloured dress. I brought in a tower of cupcakes and a confetti cannon that I planned to fire in the office to celebrate how significant this step was for me. At morning tea, Kimberley gathered everyone around and handed me the most beautiful bunch of flowers and an incredible gold container filled with notes my colleagues had written on cute note cards from one of my other favourite stationery stores, Typo. I fired the rainbow-coloured confetti in the air. It was a real celebration of my time there, and of the decision I'd made to go after what mattered most to me.

One of my colleagues who had previously given me such a hard time told me that she now believed every team needs a Michelle, a bright light who isn't afraid to make changes when it matters. It was such a turnaround and a huge compliment. It became clear to me that my journey of self-discovery had rubbed off on her. I couldn't have felt more proud of myself.

The energy I felt on that day was incredible. All the nights I had cried myself to sleep. All the frustration and moments of heartache had been worth it. I had discovered who I was and what I wanted to offer the world and I knew deep down it was going to work out. That little whisper that I had tried to ignore for so long wasn't going to let me down.

Kimberley, who had been both a friend and a confidante throughout my whole journey, took me out to lunch to celebrate. By this stage I was literally buzzing, like I had electricity coming off me. I swear the people around me could feel my happiness. I wanted to share it with everyone. To tell everyone in the street, you can have this too! I wanted everyone to know what was possible if you listened to the voice within and trusted in something bigger than yourself. It was a day I will never forget.

As we drove back to the office in Kimberley's vintage black Mini, Katy Perry's song 'By the Grace of God' came on the radio. We had both been to the Katy Perry concert together so we turned it up. As the lyrics poured out of the speakers, we both looked at each other and started bawling.

It was like my journey was being sung back to me. I chose to stay in my job and face my fears instead of running from my issues. I kept putting one foot in front of the other, my sister helping me, no more dreading going into work in the morning, allowing the universe to support me. There was that word 'grace' again, just like in the title of Mastin's book. Something had been surrounding me in those dark times and it had led me to this moment. I was so grateful.

By the time we drove back through the gates to the office carpark, 'Uptown Funk' by Bruno Mars was playing. We rolled into the carpark, singing our hearts out and dancing around in the car until the song finished. I couldn't have survived the tough moments without Kimberley, so to finish our lunch outing like this was the ultimate icing on the cake.

Scan to listen to the songs or visit michellekeating.com/shinemusic

The magic of the day didn't stop there. As I was clearing the confetti off my desk and the floor around me, Kimberley got a call from kikki.K – they were reference-checking me. What a way to end the day! Bear in mind that when I handed in my resignation eight weeks earlier, I had nothing lined up. I could hardly believe that after holding on for so long, this was how things were now unfolding for me.

I walked out of the office with my head held high. I knew I was leaving for all the right reasons. I was grateful for the lessons I had learned and the support I had received. All of it had helped set me up for the next chapter, one I was excited to write.

I celebrated over drinks with my colleagues, excited by the knowledge that the celebrations would continue with the Foo Fighters concert the following night. To acknowledge the inspiration he had given me I made a sign that I hoped to hold up for Dave Grohl that said, "Thank you for being you."

What followed was another example of serendipity at its finest. Of being in the right place at the right time. When we first arrived at the concert, my heart sank. The stage seemed miles away and I thought he's never going to see my sign. Never mind, I thought as I tucked the sign into my back pocket, I'm still going to have a great time. Then, halfway through the concert, Dave ran along a gangway to a mini stage close enough to see me and my friends in the crowd. I couldn't believe my luck. I waited in anticipation for just the right moment to hold up my sign. My heart skipped a beat as he looked over in my direction and nodded in acknowledgement. I was so thrilled to be able to thank him for the inspiration he had been to me right at the start of this journey.

I was on Cloud Nine for the rest of the weekend.

Ready to Shine

On Wednesday the following week, I followed up with kikki.K to find out what was happening with my application. I needed to know. What am I going to do with my life? Is the workshop consultant role my next thing or did I need to pursue Organised In Style?

I was over at my friend Mel's house when a phone call came through. The Head of Workshops, Sophie, told me, "We loved your story. We think you'll be a great fit for the brand so we'd love to offer you the role of Workshop Consultant!"

"YES!" I gratefully accepted and got off the phone feeling like I won the lottery to end all lotteries. I had co-created this opportunity with the universe. My dream had come true in a way that was even more incredible than I could have imagined.

At that moment it all made sense. Not getting the Dress for Success role. Not applying for the kikki.K role when I first saw it. I had needed to get into alignment with what was meant for me. All of the setbacks and challenges had actually been helping me build the foundations for my future life. One that I could now build on solid ground.

After I ended the call, Mel photographed me jumping into her swimming pool – that's how happy I was to hear the news. I couldn't remember a time that I had felt happier. I had done it. I had put myself out there and achieved something I truly wanted. I had pushed through multiple fears and made it happen. After all that struggle and grief, and the hard internal slog of figuring out who I am and what I wanted to do with my life. The feeling was incredible. It was a moment that I knew no one could ever take away from me. I had earned this. I texted everybody I could think of to share the news. I wanted to share the joy with everyone.

I couldn't wait to celebrate with Rob when he got home from work. I stopped at the supermarket to pick up a bottle of Moët champagne – we were going to fully celebrate this moment!

As I sipped the bubbly champagne, I was so excited to start my new chapter. It was the perfect combination of everything I loved. I was going to get paid to be me and run a business again.

I imagined myself standing at the bottom of my mountain. Fully prepared for the climb. I knew I had to keep on backing myself, trusting my inner voice, and following it with grace.

Finally, wonderfully, beautifully – after so many missteps and lessons, hurt and growth – l could say with confidence: I'm climbing the right mountain.

Ready to take a leap of faith?

You can pause here and go to **page 173** to complete the journaling exercises for this section.

It is not the mountain we conquer, but ourselves.

– SIR EDMUND HILLARY
NEW ZEALAND MOUNTAINEER
AND EXPLORER

Getting the job at kikki.K was one of the top moments of my life. This next chapter of my life was nothing short of miraculous. My first few months felt like an absolute dream come true. Every day felt like I was opening a new gift and the feeling of satisfaction and joy rippled out across the people in my life and the kikki.K customers who attended my workshops. I felt like I was floating so much of the time, grinning – just grinning – at how things could unfold when we trust ourselves and put our faith in something bigger than ourselves.

In one of my 'Goals' workshops, I shared my story of going to Paris to buy a pair of Christian Louboutin shoes. My story had such an impact on one of the ladies that she came along to another workshop and gave me a book: The Elves and the Shoemaker, it was a beautifully illustrated version of the fairytale featuring Manolo Blahnik shoes. Inside the book she'd written, "Thank you for reminding me about the beauty of shoes and the joy of a life well-lived."

Another workshop participant, who happens to be the most incredible opera singer, sang for us after one of the workshops, moving me and the team to tears with the beauty of what was within her. I felt so blessed to be able to encounter these incredible women and contribute to them designing and living the life of their dreams.

The first crucial step, of aligning myself with my unique path and purpose led to many more 'pinch me' experiences, including speaking in front of crowds of 100+ people, hosting my own live events, meeting the most incredible and inspiring people – including transporting the founder of kikki.K Kristina Karlsson and Tererai Trent, an international scholar, humanitarian, and educator who was named Oprah Winfrey's all-time favourite guest, in my car!

I also had the most beautiful mountain analogies and symbols come my way. Shortly after I did my first shift at kikki.K, they released a new collection all around the theme of mountains and the woman who sang the opera song later returned to the store with keyring gifts for me and the team. She gave me a carabiner, a mountain climbing tool, that had belonged to her dad. Each time I experienced moments of serendipity like this it was like a messenger saying, "You're on the right path – keep going."

It felt like every time I needed something for myself, someone would show up in my workshops with the gift, talent, or story I needed at that moment. I now understood what people mean when they say reciprocal joy – giving my full self to what I did was coming back to me tenfold. It really was the most incredible time to experience these things.

These blessings coincided almost miraculously with the continuing ups and downs of our fertility journey. Throughout that time, Rob and I continued to try and fail to conceive, experiencing another heartbreaking miscarriage, before eventually embarking on a course of IVF, which, in itself, was an emotional rollercoaster. But we never gave up hope that we would one day become parents.

Shifting from doing something that wasn't me – being a full-time employee in an unfulfilling role – to being in full alignment with my strengths, values, talents, and passions, didn't suddenly make all my problems go away. But being engaged in meaningful work gave me the strength and courage to face our fertility challenges with the same grace that I had experienced on my path to finding and doing work that I love.

When I became pregnant again from our first round of IVF, this time we continued past the point where we had lost our first two pregnancies. After finding out we were having a girl, we just knew her name had to be Grace. It was a beautiful reminder of the unconditional support that is always around us, especially in the darkest of times. The word 'grace' has continued to surround my journey, after those first few moments of meeting the universe halfway and embarking on the true path of my heart.

The lessons I learned through the process of connecting with my unique sparkle have meant that no matter the challenges I experience along the way, I'm still able to come back to that path of alignment.

A powerful example of this was on 11 March, 2020. On this life-altering day, not only did I learn that kikki.K was being placed into voluntary administration, but also that Rob was being made redundant from his Marketing Manager role.

I cried bucketloads of tears when I heard the news about kikki.K because the founders and my Australian and New Zealand teammates felt like family. I reached out to a friend who kindly met up with me so I didn't have to be alone. After sharing my disbelief and upset on a walk, I received the call from Rob. I thought he was ringing me because he had heard the news about kikki.K, but instead he was ringing me to tell me his news that he would be coming home after being let go.

I laughed – yes, laughed – when Rob told me his news because I thought, surely this must be some kind of cruel joke. I drove into the driveway with one-year-old Grace in the back, and as I parked the car, I heard the still, calm voice I'd learned to trust say, "Let it fall, you will build something from the rubble." I needed to trust that the Universe must have something bigger planned for us.

The next few weeks went by in a blur, as one after another we received crushing blows. A few days after being placed into voluntary administration, buyers had come forward with interest in purchasing kikki.K and saving the beloved brand. But a virus we've all come to know as Covid-19 began causing the shutdown of retail stores and with it, all in-person workshops.

As we went into nationwide lockdown on 25 March 2020, the fate of my livelihood was completely up in the air. But those words I heard in the car stayed with me, and as I watched countless public figures such as Brené Brown, and Kristina from kikki.K take to Instagram live to be there and support others through the uncertainty many of us were facing, the spark of an idea suddenly came to me.

What if I reached out to the people I'd connected with through my workshops and simply offered a space online where we could all support each other?

I took action and gave it a go. As I prepared for the first session, I had no idea whether my in-person workshop abilities would transfer to the online world. But a friend who I'd met through workshops, Adhirai Prema Maninilavan, offered to support the sessions and provided me with the encouragement to go live online. As the faces appeared in the boxes on screen, and we began to have conversations sharing our experiences around the world of the Pandemic, I sat back in awe of what I saw. A community was appearing before my eyes. All of us had one thing in common: We believed in the power of our dreams.

The way each of us took it in turns to support each other, I could sense something special about this gathering. We continued to meet online once a week throughout the levels of lockdown. One call even featured a surprise guest appearance from Kristina and her partner Paul from kikki.K, which brought everyone an immense amount of joy amidst the challenges we were facing.

After eight weeks of lockdown, New Zealand had successfully reduced the number of active COVID cases. We were allowed back out to connect in-person with our family and friends. But it didn't feel like the structure of support we'd created online should end. We didn't want to lose the connection we had fostered over this time.

As Rob and I were driving out to a house viewing (we'd sold our house in December 2019 and were looking to purchase another home at the time COVID restrictions came into force) I had a thought – what if we combined the community support we'd created online with a more formalised structure to help each of us keep moving towards our biggest dreams?

I excitedly shared my vision with Adhirai (also affectionately known as Adhi) of a community of women coming together to support each other to achieve our wildest dreams. Adhi agreed to come alongside me to kickstart what would be known as Dreamers Duo, which has grown into a global community called Dreamers Collective. The timing was right for me to build another business of my own, one which would be all the better from my experience at kikki.K.

In the years that have followed, one thing has stayed with me and guided me. When we show up and align ourselves with the things that bring us and others joy and meaning, there will always be support along the way.

Epilogue

There have been times since landing the job at kikki.K that have had me question and wonder if it was all just a dream. But each time I've experienced self-doubt or challenges, my ability to connect and tune into that still, small voice has encouraged me to keep going and stay the course.

The grit I developed in discovering who I was, embracing failure, and choosing to step out into uncertainty has time and time again seen me face the inevitable challenges that building a business involves. Over the years, I've nurtured a strong sense of self. I now know wholeheartedly that no matter how difficult the path, there is a way through if I listen to that voice and allow myself to learn from any mistakes or failures.

My experience of building my own brand has given me a huge appreciation for what my heroes that I've mentioned in this book have been through – from losing my co-founder (she still belongs to our Dreamers community), to having my social media hacked and having to start from scratch, to navigating the constant demands of how to balance motherhood with business, and staying true to my vision of building an empowering community to help women to confidently chase their wildest dreams.

Climbing the right mountain won't come without its challenges, nothing can completely protect you from stubbed toes, blisters, or bad weather. Having a strong sense of self, working on my resilience and continuing to trust in a force bigger than myself reminds me to embrace challenges and move through failures with a certainty that I'm on the right path. I know that as long as I keep putting one foot in front of the other, leaning on the support of my carabiner, and trusting and allowing whatever comes my way, this adventure of life will keep unfolding beautifully. The sense of satisfaction that was missing before I started listening and following my small, still voice, is now there for me time and time again.

As my journey in entrepreneurship continues, I want to assure you that the steps you take along your unique path will always be guided by grace. I hope that my story inspires you to find your own mountain and no matter where your path takes you, know that it will be the adventure of a lifetime.

This all started for me as simply a desperate desire to leave a job I no longer felt fulfilled in. What I learned and experienced along the way, including the ultimate dream outcome, has inspired me to share my experiences with others. The decision to create this journal has allowed me to reflect on the experiences and learnings that have served me in the years since. While the path ahead is not always clear, and it's rarely smooth or linear, I know this: if I could go back to that woman sitting desperately at her computer wondering if there was more to her and to her life, I would put my hand on her shoulder and whisper in her ear, "Go for it! You can do this."

Trust yourself and trust that voice. You were made for more, so go out and get it!

All my love,

Michelle x

Epilogue

My moment as the fairy princess of Auckland in the Farmers' Santa Parade, November 2005.

Cupcake Love creations, 2012.

Custom cupcakes made for Gok Wan to thank him for writing the book that gave me the courage to have another go at running my own business.

Reliving my youth at the Everclear concert, October 2012.

Epilogue | 83

My first happiness post, featuring my beloved Charlie and a couple of other posts from the month, November 2012.

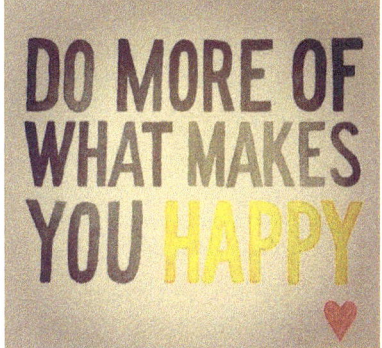

The quote and twine that inspired my happiness journey.

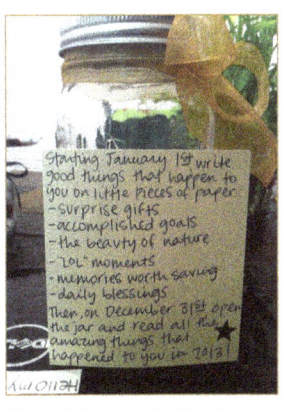

The original inspiration for my happiness jar and the end of the first year categories, 2013.

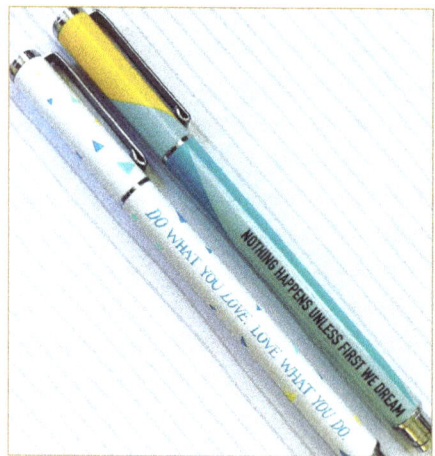

A kikki.K window display and pens kept me inspired.

A midnight BODYJAM™ class with Gandalf Archer Mills, upgrading my gym gear, and my words of thanks in the Christmas card I gave him after a year of BODYJAM™ classes.

Epilogue

Moments of happiness at my desk in the office.

Meeting Dr. John Demartini, 2013.

The Script in concert, 2013.

Some of the many quotes that inspired me on the hardest days.

 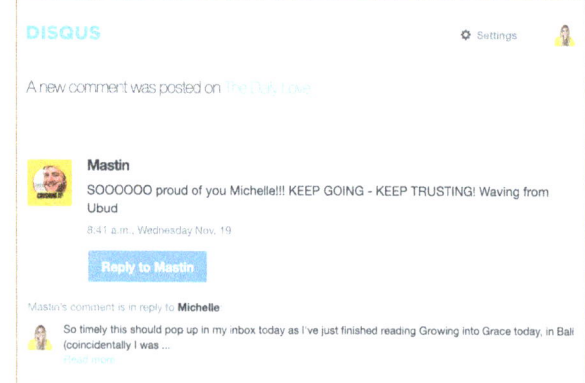

Magical Bali moments, including the pool, and my reply from Mastin Kipp, November 2014.

Epilogue | 87

My last day at work, feeling lit up like a light bulb! 21 February 2015.

Shine

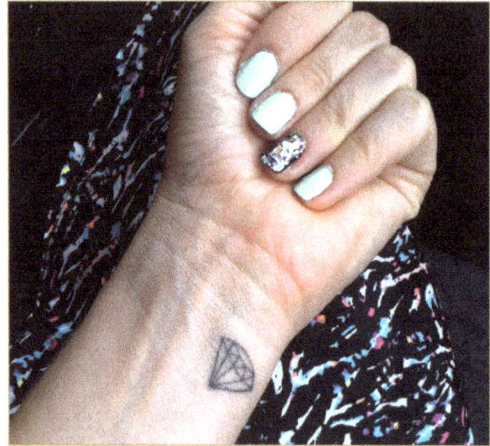

My diamond tattoo to remind me to always shine bright and never to let anyone dull my sparkle.

A (slightly blurry) photo of Dave Grohl at the February 2015 Foo Fighters concert.

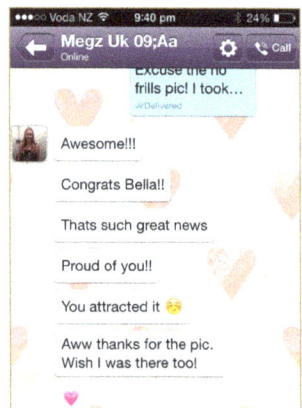

Celebrating being offered the Workshop Consultant role with kikki.K and celebrating with champagne and sharing the news with friends and family. (Bella is the nickname on of my oldest and dearest friends calls me),

Epilogue

The Facebook post celebrating my first workshop which my sister Anna attended to support me.

In action at kikki.K during a Christmas workshop.

Sharing my story at a women's event, 2019.

Meeting Kristina Karlsson, founder of kikki.K and Dr. Tererai Trent, an international scholar, humanitarian, and educator who was named Oprah Winfrey's all-time favourite guest!

Our online lockdown community.

Epilogue

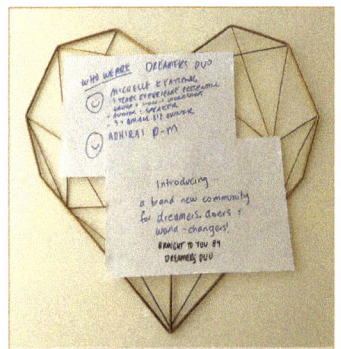
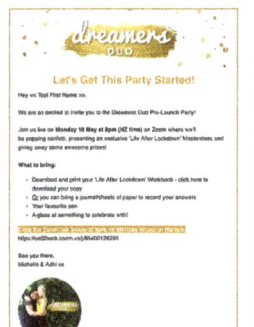
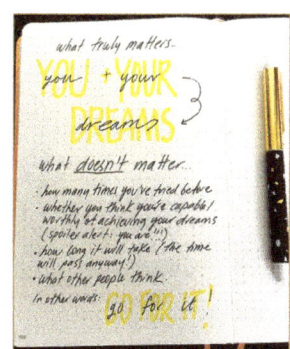

Continuing my entrepreneurial journey with Dreamers Collective.

Light up the
world by
being you.

Journaling Exercises

How to use this section

This section includes journaling prompts, exercises and resources to get you started and guide you through your own journey. By answering the questions and completing a variety of different exercises, you will gain a greater understanding of who you are and what you need to do to move forward.

I've included specific exercises along the way that will encourage you to take action. Don't skip these parts. I have no doubt you will gain insights and inspiration from reading my story and answering the prompts, but real progress will happen when you take action in your own life.

Completing these exercises will be the start of an exciting new chapter of your life. It will serve as a guide and a reminder as you work towards turning what you imagine on these pages into reality. Return to it as often as you need until you reach your desired destination.

JOURNALING EXERCISES

Do more of what makes you happy

Most of us aren't taught to focus on what makes us happy. We believe happiness is something we must earn once we've checked off enough items on our to-do list.

What would happen if you gave yourself permission to do what brings you joy? It doesn't mean shunning your responsibilities in favour of only fun things. Sometimes it can be small things – like writing down what made you smile that day.

Looking back, it was the power of deciding to do more of what made me happy that made all the difference. My visit to kikki.K, the Happiness workshop, and the happiness jar were all proactive ways to put joy front and centre in my life. I realised happiness is not something that just happens to you, but something you can choose daily.

The result? A better understanding of myself, increased energy for not only my everyday life, but also for trying to figure out what I was meant to do with my life.

30-day Happiness Challenge

Let's get your joy flowing. Inspired by the experience of reconnecting with the joy I felt as a teenager at Everclear concerts, my 30-day Happiness Challenge was a major turning point in improving my attitude towards my situation. It gave me increased confidence and energy to work towards a solution to the challenges I was facing, rather than continuing to complain to anyone who would listen.

Look for something each day that makes you happy and take a photo of it.

If you feel comfortable, share your photos on social media as a way of documenting your progress. Use the hashtag **#shinehappinesschallenge**. I'd love to see what brings you joy!

Continue this for 30 days in a row and record the difference in how you feel and how you look at the world around you.

If it feels right for you, continue the habit for another 30-60 days until looking for what makes you happy becomes a regular part of your day.

Once you have completed the challenge, write down what you learned about yourself and your happiness.

Happiness Board

One of the other ways I increased my happiness was to create a happiness board. It started as a string of twine on the wall and eventually became a pin board. I filled it with things that made me happy – the kikki.K workshop flyer, a photo of my friend's gorgeous twins and tickets from concerts I had been to. Each time I looked at it, it would remind me of all the good in my life, which gave me the energy to address everything that wasn't so good.

I invite you to create your own happiness board. It could be in physical format, like a pin board, or virtual format such as on your smartphone wallpaper/background. However you do it, make sure to fill it with things that bring you joy and enjoy the burst of energy you get from looking at it.

Answer the questions below to brainstorm ideas for what to include on yours.

Think about the things that bring you joy/make you smile.
Write a list of big and small things that make you happy.

What do you love?

Write a list of the things in the world that you love. It could be people, places, brands/companies, experiences/activities, objects or songs.

What are you drawn to?

Write a list of things that capture your attention and your heart. Perhaps it's flowers, animals, a particular type of conversation or person.

Happiness Jar

Another way of exploring your happiness is to write something that made you happy during the day on a piece of paper and put it in a jar.

1. Find a large jar. Buy or make small pieces of paper. Anything around the size of a sticky note is fine.
2. Make the jar a bit pretty with a ribbon or other decoration if you like.
3. Place the jar and paper somewhere you'll see it daily, along with a pen.
4. Every day reflect on something that made you happy. Write it down on a piece of paper. Fold it and place it in the jar.

NOTE: If you miss a few days here and there, it's totally okay. Don't worry about doing it perfectly.

BONUS EXERCISE

1. At the end of the year (or after a time period of your choosing), pull each piece of paper out and read it to remind you of each happy moment.
2. As you read each piece of paper, note what it relates to and place it in a pile. For example, it might have been exercise related, or a trip to the beach, or time spent with friends and family. These would become piles for 'exercise', 'nature' and 'time spent with loved ones'.
3. Continue adding each piece to the relevant pile until you've read them all.
4. Take a note of the largest piles and reflect on how that makes you feel. There may be some obvious ones (cuddling my cats always featured for me) and some that surprise you.
5. Pay close attention to the ones that surprise you. One of my largest piles was overcoming challenges or difficult situations at work. I was gobsmacked when I realised this, as I thought I hated being in difficult situations. But it turned out that resolving them in a way that works for everyone is something that makes me happy! Discovering this about myself meant I no longer shy away from those kinds of situations, even if being in the middle of them makes me feel uncomfortable.

Journaling Exercises | **101**

After you do this exercise, write down what you learned about yourself below.

Happiness Habits

Creating a structure in your life for activities that bring you joy and satisfaction can provide a great balance to the back and forth of growth.

As you may know from my experiences, BODYJAM™ classes and concerts were my joyful activities. They gave me something to look forward to and in different ways gave me a burst of energy and powerful insights to keep me motivated.

BODYJAM™ also gave me a safe space to fail at something. Previously, I avoided failure at all costs because it felt so painful and upsetting. Having something that was challenging but had no serious consequences if I got something wrong helped me develop the courage to take on bigger challenges and see failure in a different light.

Thinking back to your happiness lists, brainstorm ideas for happiness habits you could incorporate into your life on a regular basis.

Journaling Exercises | **103**

Create a motivational playlist

Music is something that never fails to lift my spirits. Throughout my journey I stumbled across several songs that seemed to speak to exactly where I was at and inspired me to keep going.

If you like the idea of playing music to keep you motivated, consider creating your own inspiring playlists.

Write a list of songs that pick you up, inspire you or capture how you're feeling, then add them to a playlist.

_____

_____

_____

_____

_____

_____

_____

If you'd like some inspiration to get you started, I've created a Spotify playlist with all the songs that helped me along my journey.

To access the playlist visit:
michellekeating.com/shineresources

Journaling

The fact that you have this journal is testament to how beneficial the practice of regularly putting pen to paper has been in my life.

Before I attended the kikki.K Happiness Workshop I had never written in a journal before, especially not one with guided prompts that got me to reflect on my innermost thoughts.

But once I started, I couldn't stop! Throughout the time it took me to achieve my dream of doing work that I loved, I filled countless journals with thoughts, ideas, sketches, quotes, and affirmations.

A blank journal became a constant companion of mine and I'm still an avid journaler. As well as being a great way to capture ideas and inspiration, journaling is a great way to shine a light on where you're holding yourself back and find ways to move forward again.

Below is one particular style of journaling that you might like to try.

STREAM OF CONSCIOUSNESS JOURNALING

This is particularly great if you are feeling stuck or frustrated or emotional (which by the way is totally normal).

The idea is to start with a blank page in a journal or a blank piece of paper and write whatever comes to mind about your situation. All thoughts, fears and frustrations are welcome!

Keep writing until everything is out on the page and you start to feel a shift in your thinking and gain clarity about what to do next. This kind of journaling has been a life-saver on many occasions! Some days it might take one page and others it may take three pages. The trick is to keep going until you feel a shift start to happen.

When you're finished you can either throw away the paper or simply close your journal, very rarely do I need to re-read what I've written. It's the process itself that is helpful.

Surround yourself with inspiration

I am a visual and tactile person, so I love to surround myself with imagery, quotes and objects that inspire me. This was particularly helpful when things were really challenging and I needed everything and anything to keep me going!

Inspirational quotes were particularly powerful for me. I purchased a kikki.K quote card set for my desk at work. Every morning I would choose one at random to inspire me for the day. It was uncanny how often the card I chose would be the exact words I needed to hear on that day.

I also bought two pens with quotes on them that I would write with at work and while journaling. One said: "Nothing happens unless first we dream," and the other said: "Do what you love, love what you do." The latter was the perfect reminder to keep hold of my dream while also being grateful for what I had.

What inspires you?

What physical reminders and inspiration could you surround yourself with? Brainstorm your ideas below.

Nothing can dim the light that shines from within.

JOURNALING EXERCISES

What's the work you can't not do?

Now that you've started tuning into your joy and what lights you up, it's time to discover your inner sparkle. The following exercises and resources will help you start to explore your values and strengths. You'll start to uncover how what you love can combine with what you do in a way that lights you up. When you're lit up from within, you'll light up the world around you.

sparkle

/ˈspɑːkl/

noun

1. a glittering flash of light.
"there was a sparkle in her eyes"

Similar: glitter, glint, twinkle, twinkling, flicker, flickering, shimmer, flash, shine, gleam, glow

2. vivacity and wit.
"she's got a kind of sparkle"

Similar: vivacity, animation, liveliness, vitality, life, verve, high spirits, exuberance, zest, buoyancy, effervescence, enthusiasm, energy, vigour, bounce, spirit, spiritedness, dynamism, fire, panache, drive, oomph, pizzazz, pep, zing, zip, vim, get-up-and-go

Oxford Languages

Values

Values are the things that are important to you. Each one of us has a unique set of values and these can shift and change throughout our lives. When what we do is in alignment with our values, things feel 'right'. When we are out of alignment with our values, things can feel a bit 'off'.

Identifying your values and aligning your goals with them is an important step in discovering your inner sparkle. Your values will provide clues on how to move towards doing what you love and leaving behind the things that don't align.

What do you care about? When you think about what you care about, what comes to mind? Perhaps it's creativity or creative expression. Maybe it's connection, joy, freedom, purpose or service.

Write a list of words and phrases that capture what you care about most.

What's important in your life, right now?

Your values can shift and change without us even realising it. Something that was important five years ago, may not be important now.

Write down what is really important to you in your life, right now.

What's always been important to you?

While some of our values can change over time, there may also be values that stay with you throughout your whole life. Things that are intrinsic to the person you have always been and always will be.

Write down the things that have always been important to you.

Consider how your values are already reflected in your life.

e.g. Are you big into expressing yourself through fashion? Do you value treating others with kindness? Do you like to have order and calm around you?

Who inspires you? Who do you admire?

Who makes you think: "I'd love to be like them. I'd love to do what they do. I love how they…"

What is it about your heroes that inspires you?

Do you desire a quality or character trait that they possess? Is it something they've achieved or overcome? Do they inspire you to have courage, confidence or a sense of humour?

If I look back at the people that inspired me on my journey, they all have a strong sense of purpose. They were all doing something that was a reflection of their true selves. That was what I realised was important to me too. To live a life of alignment and purpose. Once I discovered that, nothing less would suffice.

What moves you? And why?

What brings you to tears? e.g., certain TV shows, songs or even advertisements may trigger emotion in you.

For me it's watching people who are super nervous auditioning on X-Factor or the 'Got Talent' shows but end up blowing everyone away. Something about those auditions always makes me well up. Looking back, I realise that the reason I got so emotional is because that is what I wished I was doing, following my dreams regardless of how scared I felt. Pay close attention to these kinds of tears, as they are an indication of what's deeply important to you, even if you're a little afraid to acknowledge it.

If you could change anything about the world, what would it be?

What are you passionate about? Is there an injustice you'd like to resolve or a cause you would like to support. What makes you mad or fires you up that you wish you could change?

Perhaps it's to do with the environment, poverty or gender equality. It could be something on a global scale or something within your own country or community.

Now, review your answers above and see if you can see any themes emerging. Write a list of up to 10 values that you recognise are important to you.

You can capture them as words such as family, travel, security, finances, wellbeing, creativity, freedom or contribution. Or as statements such as 'feeling connected to my purpose' or 'doing something I love for a living' or 'waking up feeling energised.'

1.
2.
3.
4.
5.
6.
7.
8.
9.
10.

Looking at your answers, what in your life feels in alignment?

What feels out of alignment?

For the areas that are in alignment, is that because of conscious decisions you made and intentional action or by accident?

For the areas that are out of alignment, what changes can you make to bring them into alignment?

Strengths

Prior to learning about strengths, I thought I had to focus my energy on improving my weaknesses. In fact the opposite is true. Discovering my strengths meant I could focus on finding ways to harness what I was naturally good at. This in turn made me happier and helped me become a light in the world around me.

Your strengths play a big part in knowing where you can add the most value while also finding fulfillment within yourself – a win-win scenario for everyone!

Answer the questions below to explore your strengths.

What do you love to do?

What are you doing when you lose track of time and find yourself energised and happy?

_____

_____

_____

_____

_____

_____

_____

_____

What are you naturally good at and enjoy doing?

We can all learn to be good at things, but it doesn't necessarily mean we enjoy doing them. Think about activities and tasks that make you feel energised even after you've been doing them for a while. It could be inside or outside of work. Are you great with people, love cooking, have a passion for music or are you a genius at organising people or events?

What do people regularly compliment you on?

Especially if it's outside of your role or job description. What do people say "thank you" for and appreciate that you do naturally? What do others ask you for help with that you enjoy doing?

What are you naturally drawn to?

What do you find yourself doing in a team or a group, even if no one asks you to do it?

What's the work you can't not do?

I love this question from Scott Dinsmore's 'How to find work you love' TEDx Talk.

If there is anything you can't not do in your life, write it down below.

Now, review your answers and see if you can see any themes emerging. Write a list of up to five strengths that you recognise come naturally to you.

e.g. Big picture thinking, communicating with others, empathising with people.

1.

2.

3.

4.

5.

Extra resources

VALUE DETERMINATION PROCESS

If you'd like to dive deeper into your values, I highly recommend checking out the **Demartini Value Determination Process.**

Dr. Demartini was a huge inspiration for me to embrace what was *actually* important to me, not what I thought should make me happy. I recommend taking the free online assessment to help you get clear on your values and what makes you shine.

He also has written a book called **The Values Factor** which goes into more detail and has some great exercises to explore your values even further.

STRENGTHS

If you'd like to explore your strengths further, below are a few resources that I recommend taking a look at.

TROMBONE PLAYER WANTED

This video series by Marcus Buckingham, a leader in the field of using your strengths at work, is a great introduction to the power of understanding your strengths. You can find it on YouTube by searching Trombone Player Wanted.

CLIFTONSTRENGTHS® ASSESSMENT

Understanding my strengths through this paid online assessment helped me understand a lot more about who I was and how I could embrace my uniqueness. It helped me appreciate what I was naturally good at, how I could benefit others with my natural strengths and why some things drained me even though I was good at them.

MY FAVOURITE TED TALKS

How to Find Work You Love – Scott Dinsmore

The Skill of Self Confidence – Dr. Ivan Joseph

How to Know Your Life Purpose in 5 Minutes – Adam Leipzig

Grit: The Power of Passion and Perseverance – Angela Lee Duckworth

Start With Why – Simon Sinek

Love is The Key & Backward Business Plan – Caitlin Crosby

The Power of Vulnerability & Why Your Critics Aren't The Ones Who Count – Brené Brown

TIP: You can pretty much type any word into the YouTube search bar before the word TED Talk and you'll get dozens of options to choose from. e.g. Purpose Ted Talk

To access links to these resources, scan the QR code or visit
michellekeating.com/shineresources

Bringing it together

By now you should be starting to get a clearer picture about what really lights you up. By stepping back and looking at the things that reflect your uniqueness, you can start to look at how you can bring it all together and start moving towards doing something that matches who you truly are.

Imagine you could do absolutely anything you wanted in life. What would that be?

Don't worry about the 'how', e.g., the qualifications, experience or what it might take to make it happen. Do you long to be an entrepreneur, a singer, an artist? Even if it's miles apart from what you are currently doing, write it below.

Complete this sentence: I wish I could get paid to…

While exploring ideas for myself, I said to a workmate, "I wish I could get paid to talk!" I'd initially brushed it off thinking that could never be possible. Little did I know I'd eventually end up presenting and facilitating workshops and, in fact, be paid to talk!

I wish I could get paid to

Are there any unrealised childhood dreams you still have?

Is there something you wished you could have done when you were younger but didn't get the chance to pursue it?

Is there anything you're afraid to write down because it feels too big?

Don't worry if something feels completely unachievable. If it comes to mind, write it down.

This following question is particularly important. You may feel uncomfortable but please don't skip it.

What would you love to do but you're worried you can't do it?

Maybe it's something you feel you've tried and failed at before or it feels too late to go for it.

Light up the world by being you

Hopefully you'll be starting to get clear on what it is you really want. Don't worry if it still feels a bit vague at the moment. I started with simply knowing that I wanted to be in business. I had no idea what kind of business, but I knew the direction I was heading in and that was enough to get started.

It's also okay if you have absolutely no idea whether you could achieve it or how to go about making it a reality. Don't be afraid of what anyone else might think of it. Don't edit it because it may feel too big (or too small). And if actually writing it down scares the wits out of you, that's a good sign, trust me!

Write down how you would love to light up the world with your unique sparkle.

How I will light up the world by being me:

Repeat after me:
Progress not perfection
Progress not perfection
Progress not perfection

JOURNALING EXERCISES

The Messy Middle

You are on your way. You have ignited a dream in your heart and no doubt you are excited to turn it into reality.

This phase can come with a sense of push and pull. Your dream and vision for what you want will pull you forward, while at the same time you may feel yourself being pushed back into old ways of thinking and acting.

During this constant internal battle, the pull towards my dream of being in business and the push back to my old way of thinking, I was building my determination, stamina, and toolkit. I have a mantra: 'it's messy in the middle'. When I look back, I realise that this often painful period of waiting and transition was polishing my sparkle. The whole experience of to-ing and fro-ing made it feel more urgent and important to take that bold leap of leaving my job and pursuing my passion for business.

To counteract this natural occurrence when you're working towards making a big change in your life, it's wise to put some supports in place to remind you of where you are heading and to help keep you on track when things try to pull you back.

Remind yourself of your destination

When I went to see Irish band The Script in concert and felt uplifted by their song 'Hall of Fame', I wrote the words 'every day is one step closer to my dream job' on a whiteboard in our pantry. This visual reminder inspired me every time I reached for a snack or was in the kitchen.

Complete the sentence for your dream in the space below:

Every day is one step closer to

Transfer the sentence you wrote above onto a piece of card or onto something similar.

I have designed a printable card that you can print out and fill in to complete this step.

**You can download it here:
michellekeating.com/resources**

CHOOSE A LOCATION YOU LOOK AT DAILY

It could be on the fridge, in the pantry, in your wardrobe or on your screensaver. Choose somewhere you feel comfortable displaying it and somewhere you will see it on a daily basis.

Speak your new reality into existence

Imagine you are at lunch with friends and you have the opportunity to share what you do. What would you say? Use the space below to write down some ideas about how you might share your vision for your life in a sentence or two.

After my 'Walt Disney moment' when people asked what I did, I would say: "I work as a graphic designer, but I want to run my own business." My whole language started to change, and I put my dreams at the forefront. I vividly remember the first time I tried this out at a good friend's birthday lunch. With as much confidence as I could muster, I said it to a couple I had just met and to my delight neither of them laughed in my face. It might sound silly, but that moment was hugely impactful to me. They took what I said at face value and believed me. It was a turning point. I was beginning to leave my old identity behind me and forge a new one that felt right to me.

EXERCISE

Share your dream with at least five people over the next month. Whenever the opportunity arises to share what you're working towards, take it. Don't worry about someone making fun of you or not believing in you. It's all about practice and you never know who might become your biggest cheerleader!

Your support crew

Courage can be borrowed. For a long time on my journey I had very little faith and belief in myself. I had developed an unshakeable belief in my dream thanks to the examples I had surrounded myself with, but my belief in myself was a little shaky. After all, I felt like I had proven to myself twice that I was rubbish at business, so I certainly wasn't brimming with confidence in my ability.

Yet as I tentatively started to share my dream with people close to me, something wonderful happened. A few of my friends and family members actually believed I was capable of doing it!

These people became my cheerleaders. The people who believed in me even when I didn't believe in myself.

My sister Anna would send me links to resources that could help me. My friend Angela would send me encouraging messages and inspiring videos. Another friend Vanessa would sit with me for hours at a time, providing space for me to voice my fears and work through them. My husband Rob would send me perfectly timed quotes on my worst days. I had two friends called Kate, one who bought me the most perfect inspirational gifts and the other who would sit with me over brunch after the gym some Saturdays. Our post BODYJAM™ chats made me believe I was capable of so much more, even if I didn't feel like I had proof – yet.

The cheerleaders in your life may not be who you expect, but when you discover them, lean on their belief while you build belief in yourself.

Our dreams and self-belief can feel a little fragile at times, so having other people who remind you of your ability is a powerful antidote in these moments.

List the people in your life that believe in you no matter what.
Consider sharing your dream with them and ask for their support.

Quieten the 'what-ifs'

While I was inspired by my desired outcome, it didn't stop somewhat irrational fears from surfacing. I'd be happily day-dreaming about leaving my job and then bam! – an unhelpful thought would surface and derail my confidence and commitment.

Thoughts like, what if I'm really not good enough? What if I do this and we can't pay our bills? What if I try and fail, again? These thoughts would paralyze me from taking action and made it hard to concentrate on what I knew I needed to do.

Eventually, I found writing down my fears and analysing them more critically helped to bring some rationality to them and I found ways to move forward, despite having these fears.

List any fears you're feeling about taking action towards what you want?

One of the most influential books I read throughout this time was **The 4-Hour Work Week** by Timothy Ferriss. It's such a great book for challenging your thinking and one of the activities called 'Fear-Setting' is particularly helpful if you have a real fear of what might happen if you pursue your dreams.

To try it out, Google 'Fear-Setting by Timothy Ferriss' or visit michellekeating.com/shineresources to access the link.

Re-energise yourself and build your belief

At the time my daily commute was generally an hour each way, sitting in bumper to bumper traffic. I didn't have a huge amount of time outside of work to focus on my dream. But because I was determined I was going to somehow make this work, I turned my morning and afternoon commute into an opportunity to learn and be inspired.

I would listen to TED Talks, podcasts, YouTube clips and occasionally read an inspiring book on my Kindle while waiting in the long queue at the lights to get onto the motorway (don't tell anyone I told you that)! On the awful days I blasted my motivational playlist on my way home and sang my heart out behind the wheel, often in between crying tears of frustration too.

These moments became a motivating bookend to my day, when I could fantasise about what it would be like to leave my job while also learning and being inspired by people who would help me get there.

I've included a list of my favourite inspiring books and videos on the next page to get you started.

My List of Inspiration

BOOKS

The Gifts of Imperfection, Daring Greatly & Rising Strong – Brené Brown

Everything is Figureoutable – Marie Forleo

The Bear Necessities of Business: Building a Company with Heart – Amy Joyner and Maxine Clark (Founder of Build a Bear)

500 Words of Wisdom – Sarah Liu

The Martha Rules: 10 Essentials for Achieving Success as you Start, Grow or Manage a Business – Martha Stewart

Through Thick and Thin – Gok Wan (this one was a huge inspiration for me to continue my business journey)

YOUTUBE CLIPS/CHANNELS

Steve Jobs' 2005 Stanford University commencement speech

MarieTV – Marie Forleo

What is the next right move? – Oprah Winfrey

MOVIES

'Walt Before Mickey'
This Netflix movie tells the story of what happened in Walt's first businesses and his journey to creating Mickey Mouse. It's such an inspiring watch!

To access links to my inspiration list, visit michellekeating.com/shineresources

Review your current situation

As much as I wanted to, I understood that I wouldn't be able to just up and leave my job and expect to replace my entire income with a new business straight away.

I thought it would be wise to start putting aside money to help fund my dream and allow me to eventually leave my job and continue to pay the bills while I established something of my own.

I also knew that my situation at work felt unbearable at times so I needed to do something to keep my spirits up and energy high while I slowly but surely moved towards my goal of leaving my 9 to 5 for good.

By using these insights, I was then able to make some changes in my everyday life that would support me to make progress while still surviving the daily grind.

Here's what I did:

ADJUST MY SPENDING, CREATE A BUDGET AND START SAVING

I had developed unhelpful spending habits to escape how I was feeling. I spent a lot of money on things like pretty stationery and going out for dinner and drinks as a distraction.

With my newfound motivation, instead of spending time and money going out as much as I had been, I started to invest money into things that would help me grow. I bought courses, books, and tickets to events that I felt would help me get closer to my goal, instead of just temporarily distracting myself from my situation at work.

I also addressed my habit of going shopping to make myself feel better after a bad day at work. I realised that while it made me feel good in the moment, once the excitement of buying something new wore off, I was back to feeling crap about my situation. Ultimately it was a short-term fix not a long-term solution.

However, I knew that depriving myself completely was not going to work either, so I made sure that I still had a (much smaller) budget to buy things that brought me joy. This at the time was beautiful stationery and visits to kikki.K.

My much more modest budget each month still gave me a treat to look forward to while allowing me to save money for when I eventually went out on my own.

Review your current situation and habits. Brainstorm the changes you could make to help support your dream.

Make a list of actions to take to make these changes in your life

For example, I knew I needed to curb my impulse spending by creating a realistic budget that allowed for both saving and spending on the occasional treat, which meant creating a budget and setting up a savings account.

Get around people doing what you want to do

Soon after acknowledging that I really wanted to be in business, I signed-up to a women in business event in my local area. I felt like a bit of a fraud as I didn't yet have another business. But I signed up anyway so I could be around the kinds of people I wanted to become.

Towards the end of the event. I started to recognise the owners of businesses that I had seen advertised in local publications and secretly admired. I stood back and listened in on some of the conversations that were going on.

The conversations ranged from sharing about challenges with hiring staff, struggles to get sales and marketing mishaps. I couldn't believe what I was hearing! You mean these women who I admired and thought had it all together because they were running what I saw as successful businesses weren't doing it perfectly?!

It was a big moment for me, as I had been so hard on myself for the mistakes I made in my first two businesses that I almost hung up my business hat forever. It was another reminder that no matter how successful someone looks on the outside, it doesn't mean they don't make mistakes and it certainly doesn't mean they're doing it perfectly.

As well as boosting my confidence, attending events was a great opportunity to learn from experts and meet like-minded people.

Look for events you could attend

List the types of events you might like to attend. For example: conferences, meetups, events with live speakers.

TIP: Once you have your list, research upcoming events in your area or region. If you find one you like the sound of, grab a ticket and go along.

Practice gratitude

If you find yourself feeling particularly down or frustrated about your situation, practising gratitude for your situation is a powerful way to shift your focus and renew your energy.

Not long into my journey of researching and moving towards getting back into business for myself again, I came across a book called **Click Millionaires** by Scott Fox.

I devoured it in one sitting over the weekend and became inspired by the idea of creating an internet business, like so many of the success stories in the book. Stories of people who had turned their passion into a paying blog or website and who were living the life I dreamed of.

I was fired up by reading these stories and felt like I was onto a winner. I imagined the possibilities all weekend and practically waltzed into work on the Monday thinking I had a ticket out of my situation.

About ten minutes later the reality of having to do the job I didn't like for yet another week sunk in. I felt a sinking feeling in my stomach and all the excitement from the weekend drained away.

I recalled Dr. Demartini explaining in the Master Planning for Life course how feelings of sadness and depression can be a signal to pay attention to. His theory was that we can feel down or depressed when we have unrealistic expectations (or fantasies as he called them) that don't measure up to our reality. An accurate description of how I was feeling.

By listing the drawbacks of your fantasy or unrealistic expectations, as well as a list of the benefits of your current reality, you can balance your thinking and feel grateful for being where you are, not where you wish you were.

Let's use my Click Millionaires experience as an example.

My fantasy or unrealistic expectation was that reading a book would change my life in a weekend.

My reality was that I still had the same job I did before reading the book. And while I was fired up by the idea of an internet business, it most certainly wasn't going to happen overnight, no matter how much I wished it would.

When I recognised that this was what was making me feel down and depressed, I took some time to make two lists on a piece of paper.

1. *The benefits of my current reality (what was good about being where I was currently).*
2. *The drawbacks of my fantasy being real (the downsides to having what I wanted instantly).*

As I added thoughts to each list, I realised that fast forwarding to a successful business would mean I would potentially miss out on the growth needed to sustain a business long term.

I also reminded myself that while I wasn't where I wanted to be yet, I could still be grateful for the income from my job that allowed me to do the fun things I enjoyed and for the support I was receiving from friends and family to help me work through my situation.

I could feel my self-confidence come back. It was like an elixir for my feelings of frustration.

If you find yourself feeling depressed or despondent, I highly recommend giving Dr. Demartini's exercise a try.

To access the link, visit
michellekeating.com/shineresources

This is for you.
Don't
give
up.

JOURNALING EXERCISES

By now, you'll be on your way to closing the gap from where you are and where you want to be. Remember, the journey is about progress, not perfection. As long as you keep showing up, trust that you are making progress. With the right preparation, action and support systems in place, your life will start to transform in the most amazing ways.

However, with this exciting growth can also come resistance. You might feel like you're almost there and then boom! Your negative self-talk goes up a notch, all the reasons that you shouldn't take action start to bubble up in your brain and suddenly it seems way more appealing to clean the house than work on your dream.

While it may make you feel like you want to stop and give it all up, this resistance can actually be a good thing. It's a sign that you're at the edge of your comfort zone and guess what, amazing things are waiting for you on the other side. When you understand resistance you can work with it and use it as fuel to achieve the breakthroughs necessary to start living your dreams on a daily basis.

In this section I'll share tools and strategies to help keep the faith and continue to take courageous action despite any resistance, to ultimately produce the outcomes you desire, which may just eventuate in a way that is even more amazing than you've been imagining!

Meditation

I highly recommend including meditation in your daily routine. By now you'll have a vision of what you want, but, if you're like I was, you're battling a mental list of your history of 'failures'. Reasons why you're not qualified or experienced enough, and other reasons to back up why you shouldn't move forward. Left unchecked, this can take you out of the game.

I found daily meditation a great way to reconnect with my vision and help me make it through the day feeling calm and focused.

If meditation is completely new to you, here's a simple way to practice it, or you can also find many amazing apps and guided meditations online.

1. Pick a quiet spot where you won't be interrupted.
2. My favourite place at the time was on our front lawn in the morning before I got ready for work. Often during my meditations one or both of our cats would join me for snuggles, which I loved.
3. Set a timer for 10 minutes, close your eyes and begin to focus on your breath.
4. Breathe deeply in and slowly out until the timer goes off.
5. If thoughts come to your mind, acknowledge them and bring your focus back to your breath.
6. Over time and with regular practice, not only does meditation help calm any stress or anxiety you may be feeling, but it also helps you tune into your intuition and inner wisdom.
7. As you continue to concentrate on your breath, you may start to notice inspired thoughts. The small, still voice within that knows what you truly want and believes you can have it.
8. Pay attention to this voice, these are the whispers of your soul speaking to you.

Only you have your unique dream in your heart. This practice will help you reconnect with your dream regularly and guide you to take a particular action. When you act on those nudges, it's amazing where they can lead you.

Setting a deadline

One of the most impactful things you can do at this stage is to set yourself a deadline of when you'd like to achieve your dream.

Committing to a date has several benefits:

- It gives you something concrete to work towards
- You can work backwards from the date to work out what needs to happen, by when and in what order
- It gives you the motivation to do something NOW!

Believe it or not, it took me ages to commit to a deadline, which made leaving my job feel like a someday dream. So instead of making progress, I spent a lot of time outside of work complaining about it. When I finally committed to a date, it set in motion things that I would have otherwise kept putting off.

The idea of setting a date in this phase is to fully commit to what you want, even if it feels scary. Whether you hit it or miss it is not as important as having something concrete to work towards.

Take a moment to think about how long it might potentially take you to achieve your dream and fill in the blanks below to commit to a date.

It is _____ _____ _____

            (day)   (month)   (year)

I have achieved my dream of

Commit to your success

Now that you have a date locked in, let's do something significant to cement your future outcome. For me it was typing up my resignation letter with the date I had chosen. While I ended up choosing to shift the date to approximately six months later, the act of committing to a date set the wheels in motion for me to face challenges and take actions that lead to my eventual success.

Brainstorm ideas for a significant action you could take to fully commit to your end goal.

Pick something that feels outside your comfort zone but still allows you time to get your ducks in a row.

Write a letter from your future self

Imagine you have achieved your dream. What do you want the present you to know?

Write down everything you may need to hear to keep going when the days are tough.

What encouragement might you need? What words would help you keep going? Read this as often as you need throughout your journey.

A NOTE ABOUT INVESTING IN YOURSELF

Don't be afraid to invest in yourself and your growth. While there are a lot of great free resources out there, I've noticed that each time I invested in myself I upleveled faster. It started off as a small investment in the CliftonStrengths® Assessment and grew into more significant investments in courses and programmes such as Dr. Demartini's **Master Planning for Life** and Marie Forleo's **B-School.**

The big investments felt incredibly scary, but the return on investment was huge. If you have the means, investing in yourself wisely can fast-track your progress. It also opens you up to awesome networks of like-minded people who can support your progress.

Make time to work on your dream

Depending on your situation, you may have a lot of time to dedicate or only a small amount. How much time you have available isn't important, what is important is making sure you establish a routine that allows you to regularly sit down and make progress.

I was working at least 40 hours per week, so for me, it was on Saturday afternoons after my BODYJAM™ class. I would position myself on a lounger on our deck and commit to taking some kind of action. Sometimes it was completing coursework, sometimes it was reading a book about a business owner or company I admired and sometimes it was doing some research. Ultimately, it didn't matter what it was I was doing. What mattered was that I was doing something.

My beautiful friend Kate had a knack of giving me presents that inspired me to keep going. I still have the Anything Is Possible tote bag she gave me, and I put the plaque she gifted me that said, 'Dream lofty dreams, and as you dream, so shall you become' on the wall on our deck so I could look up at it every time I sat down to make progress on my dreams.

I didn't manage to do this every single Saturday, but over time it became a habit and something that I started looking forward to as it gave me a sense of accomplishment and having some control over my destiny.

> *It's important that you have some kind of dedicated time set in stone that you try your very best to adhere to. It may take a few tries to figure out what works best for you, so don't worry if it doesn't fall into place immediately. Keep experimenting until you find something that works for you.*

Take a look at your current schedule and pick a day and time that you are going to put aside to work on your dream.

Write the day(s) and time(s) below and then schedule them into your diary.

Now, ask yourself, is there anything that needs to change in my life to allow this to happen?

It goes without saying that I don't expect you to do this perfectly. Because life will happen and things we inevitably get in the way occasionally. That's okay. However, think about anything you may need to stop or start doing to ensure you have time you can dedicate on a regular basis.

Journaling Exercises | **157**

If you'd like some extra support and accountability, Dreamers Collective has regular online sessions designed to help you dedicate time to work on your biggest dreams.

To find out more about Dreamers Collective visit michellekeating.com/shineresources

Learn from others

Another way to fast-track your progress is to speak to people who have already done what you are setting out to do.

People who have succeeded in doing something they love are generally happy to share their experiences and what they've learnt to inspire and encourage others to give it a go.

It could be someone you know that is doing something you'd love to do. Or perhaps someone you follow on social media. It doesn't matter whether they are two steps or ten steps ahead of you. What matters is that they have experience in doing what you want to do!

Soon after I decided I wanted to be in business again, I reached out to a friend who I knew had successfully run a business for several years. I took him out for coffee and shared what I was hoping to do and asked for his advice. It was so inspiring to sit with someone who was living the life I dreamed of and so valuable to be able to ask specific questions.

It also reminded me that everyone who has succeeded long term has faced challenges and had moments of doubt along the way. I was reassured that doing things perfectly was not a prerequisite for long term success.

Write a list of anyone who you could contact for ideas, advice and inspiration.

They may be people you already know, people you've heard about or people you admire. It might be a type of person you could look up on the internet. For example, yoga instructors in your area.

Brainstorm questions you'd like to ask

Maybe you want to hear about their story, or what advice they might have for someone starting out. Jot down any ideas that come to mind.

Brainstorm ideas on how you could get in touch with them for a conversation

If you know them already, perhaps it's as simple as sending a message asking whether they would meet for coffee or have a phone conversation with you. If it's someone doing something you want to do, send them an email or call them to see if you can ask them some questions. If it's someone really well known you could take a chance and send them a personal note, you never know what might happen!

Journaling Exercises | **161**

Choose at least five people you want to contact and fill in the table below with their details. Then commit to reaching out to at least 2-3 people off your list this coming week to ask them for their advice/help.

WHO WILL I CONTACT?	WHAT DO I WANT TO ASK THEM?	HOW WILL I CONTACT THEM?

Don't get disheartened if someone says no or you can't get in contact with them. Keep going until someone says yes. Also, if someone does give their time and shares their expertise with you, be sure to express your gratitude. Perhaps pay for their lunch or coffee or send them a personal thank you note afterwards.

Use the space below to write notes about anything you learn from these conversations. If there are any actions to take that come out of your conversations, make a note of them here so you can work through them during the time you've set aside to work on your dreams.

Role models

Of course, if someone on your list is famous and highly sought after, you may find it difficult to access them. If that's the case, there are plenty of other ways that you can learn from them. For example: they may have written a book, been interviewed on a podcast or for a magazine, featured in a documentary or they may share their journey via social media. They may even speak at events or host workshops or courses you can attend.

While your sparkle is unique, surrounding yourself with, and learning from examples of what's possible, helps to boost your belief and gain insights and knowledge about how to make your dream a reality too.

Learning about the experiences, the challenges overcome and the lessons learned along the way by people I admire, always leaves me feeling that if it's possible for them, it might very well be possible for me too.

Once I started looking, I discovered all kinds of people who were living my dream and pursued ways to learn from them.

If you can't connect directly with someone on your list to contact, consider other ways you can learn from them.

Brainstorm your ideas below. If there are any actions you want to take, write them down here so you can work on them during the time you've set aside to work on your dreams.

Peers and finding your village

Sometimes it might feel like you're the only one struggling with a million thoughts and worries while everyone around you looks like they have it all together. Trust me when I say you are not alone in how you're feeling.

I remember feeling like the odd one out in my job. I wondered whether I should just get on with it and be grateful for what I had instead of trying hard to do something different. I obviously couldn't share how I was feeling with colleagues and even some of my closest friends couldn't relate to what I was going through.

When my sister suggested I sign up for Marie Forleo's B-School and I joined the Facebook group, I felt like I had found my tribe. All of a sudden, I was surrounded by others that felt exactly the same way and shared the same vision of being in business. I was ecstatic! I no longer felt alone and had a whole support network of people to cheer me on and give me valuable support and advice.

If what you want to achieve is outside the realm of your existing network of friends and family, I highly recommend finding a community of like-minded people who 'get it' that you can share your journey with. Before long they'll probably end up feeling like a second family!

List the ways you can surround yourself with other people on the same journey as you.

It could be online groups, in-person meetups or you could even create your own community with people you know.

Mirrors

At one point I muttered "F you" under my breath to my workmates. Now I can honestly say "thank you" for how they helped me move beyond my limits into a bigger version of myself.

If, on your journey, you come across someone that triggers strong emotions in you, I want you to know this: Those that trigger you the most, teach you the most.

Let me say that again: those that trigger you the most, teach you the most.

Now, I'm not for a minute saying you should put up with any kind of behaviour that is physically or emotionally abusive. However, if there is a theme to the kind of behaviour you are attracting that is frustrating you but not affecting your safety, there's an opportunity to dig deeper and find out how you can use this as feedback to grow.

Think of it as life conspiring to remind you of your greatness and what you really want. Perhaps if my situation at work hadn't been so bad, I wouldn't have been so motivated to move on. It was like everyone around me was secretly communicating, "We know you don't want to be a graphic designer, so just admit it. Go for your dream already!"

When you take the view that everything around you is happening for you, not to you, you have the power to make changes that will ultimately serve your goal. You can't change others, but you can change yourself!

In hindsight, the insights I gained on reflecting on the interactions with my colleagues, as challenging as they were at the time, has stood me well in the world of entrepreneurship. It built my courage and awareness around not just focusing on the good things and has helped me embrace challenges as opportunities for growth.

Are there any people in your life that are triggering a strong emotional response in you? Ask yourself, what are these people teaching me and how can I use this to help me achieve my dream?

Where in your life might you be avoiding responsibility?

Ask yourself: are external conflicts highlighting areas where I'm not taking full responsibility for my life and how can I use this knowledge to help me achieve my dream?

ACTIVITY

Double-sided letter

This is something I learned from one of my beloved kikki.K workshop attendees and I find it really helpful if a situation is churning in my head or I'm feeling in a bit of a funk about something or someone. I wish I'd had access to it earlier, so I want to include it for you as a resource.

1. Grab a sheet of paper that can be written on both sides.
2. At the top of one side write 'Dear (insert person or situation you want clarity on or you are having difficulty with)'
3. Next, write a letter to the person or situation expressing your thoughts, feelings and concerns as they come to you. There is no need to censor anything or worry about hurting anyone's feelings.
4. When you're done, sign off with your name.
5. Then turn the sheet of paper over and write 'Dear (insert your name)' at the top.
6. Intuitively write a reply to yourself from the person or situation. Don't worry if you're not sure exactly what they would say, simply put pen to paper and write everything that comes to mind.
7. When you're finished, sign off with their name/the situation.

Once complete, you should have a greater sense of perspective on the situation and one or two new ways to approach it. While it may sound a little strange at first, I highly recommend giving this a go!

Dealing with disappointment

At some point in your journey, it's likely your plan or action steps won't unfold how you want them to. This can be disheartening for even the strongest person pursuing a dream. It might feel like you're almost there, like things are lining up nicely, and your dream is just within reach. Then, bam! For some reason it doesn't work out.

Allowing myself to really feel the disappointment made me realise just how badly I wanted to achieve my goal. Not getting what I wanted and acknowledging how disappointed I felt served to solidify my commitment to my dream. While it was certainly no fun going through it at the time, it helped me see just how important my dream was to me.

Try these tips for processing and moving through disappointment.

Feel all the feels. Any number of feelings may arise when things don't go to plan for you. Allow yourself to feel all of it. Do whatever you need to do – cry, scream, eat all the ice cream. Give yourself the time and space you need. Giving myself time to really feel the disappointment when I wasn't hired by Dress for Success, and missing my planned resignation date, was a painful but crucial step for me. By accepting how I felt, I allowed the pain to propel me forward, but only once I had given myself permission and time to really feel the emotions.

Trust the process. Just because it didn't go according to your plan, trust that it's going according to a bigger plan. Remind yourself that wherever you are right now is where you're meant to be.

Get support. Talk to someone who knows your dream and who will support you no matter how long it takes you to achieve it. When you're ready, reach out to your cheerleaders or your peers and share how you are feeling. It's more than okay to throw your toys and have a vent and a cry with someone you trust and who loves you.

Try to see it as a stepping stone to success. While the dictionary definition of failure is lack of success, it doesn't necessarily mean you didn't succeed. Look for the successes in all your attempts. Yes, I hadn't secured a new role by the time I wanted to hand in my resignation. But I'd handled the tense situation I had been avoiding at work. I'd grown as a person in the process.

Look for the learning. What did you learn about yourself? Your situation? Try and look for something positive in the experience. On reflection, I realised that while it seemed like a move in the right direction, deep down I didn't want to work for another company. I really did want to go into business again.

Lean on the tools and habits you've already developed. Find ways to lift your spirits and clear any stuck energy or feelings you may have around the experience before you try again. Listen to music, look at your favourite quotes for inspiration or dance it out. I find journaling particularly helpful when I'm feeling flat and things haven't gone to plan.

Don't give up. Look at how you can use this experience to keep moving towards your ultimate goal. Take the lessons, keep your heart open and your dream alive. You never know, something amazing may be just around the corner.

When the days are tough and you think you'll never get there, remember this: Pressure makes diamonds!

JOURNALING EXERCISES

A leap of faith

At some point you might decide it's time to take a leap of faith, to throw caution to the wind and trust that the universe will catch you. You will know if and when this is right for you. You may find that a gradual transition is better for you, and that's great too.

A leap of faith is a moment of surrender. It's about trusting that all the work you've done has laid a foundation. It's about choosing to lean into your intuition and being open for the magic to unfold!

If you feel that taking a giant leap towards your heart's desire is the right move for you, here are my recommendations for preparing for and taking a leap of faith.

Getting unstuck

If you feel like you're doing all the right things but for some reason you can't move forward, I highly recommend doing this exercise to reveal what may be keeping you stuck. I am forever grateful for Jen Stemp for sharing this exercise via her email newsletter.

1. In a notebook, write three possible scenarios/options for your circumstances.
2. List the pros and cons for each of the options in columns below each option. Aim for 5–10 pros and cons for each scenario.
3. Reflect on your answers and see whether you can determine what is really holding you back from making a move.
4. Brainstorm ways you can move forward with these new insights.

> *I realised that even though I felt certain about my desire to be in business, the sense of safety and security I was getting from the job was keeping me stuck. That was it! I knew what I wanted but I didn't fully believe in myself yet. I was afraid to let go of the safety net.*

EXAMPLE

OPTION 1: STAY IN MY JOB		OPTION 2: GET ANOTHER JOB / GO CONTRACTING		OPTION 3: START A BUSINESS	
Pros	**Cons**	**Pros**	**Cons**	**Pros**	**Cons**
Stable income	Limited flexibility	Could choose something that is more aligned	Won't solve the issue of feeling like I want to do more with my life	Flexibility and freedom, not tied to a desk for 8 hours a day	Irregular income
Buy what I want and do what I want	**Doing tasks I don't want to do**				**Potentially work more hours than a job**
Security	No passion for what I'm doing	Stable income while working on my business dreams	May end up facing the same challenges that I have just overcome	**Choose what I want to do and who to work with**	No guarantees it will work
Eligible for maternity pay				Self-expression	**Need to be self-motivated**

Leap of faith checklist

Use the checklist below to determine whether taking a leap of faith could be your next best step...

- ☐ I've taken the time to get crystal clear on the reality of what it is I want (the good, the bad and the ugly) and feel prepared to support myself financially and emotionally.

- ☐ I've faced my current fears, perfectionism and circumstances (including people) along the way and now there is nothing or no-one holding me back, except myself.

- ☐ I've got a plan, and I'm comfortable if it needs adjusting along the way.

- ☐ I'm more concerned about chasing my dream than what anyone else thinks of me.

- ☐ I'm willing to let go and listen to my intuition, and trust it to lead the way.

Always shine bright and never let anyone dull your sparkle.

Final words of encouragement

In the dark is where you'll find your light. If it feels hard, like it's taking too long and you're not good enough, remember you are in the right place. Pressure makes diamonds.

It is during this time that you are becoming who you need to be for the next phase of your life. Yes, it may feel hard, but it's no harder than living a life that isn't a match for who you know yourself to be.

I want you to know that whatever you go through to get this far will be exactly what you need to carry you through the next phase, when you are climbing your mountain.

You will discover the power of your inner sparkle, and no one can ever take that away from you.

Keep the faith and know that brighter days will come. Keep shining bright, and never let anyone dull your sparkle!

This is not the end of our journey together, it's just the beginning! I would love to support you and celebrate your success as you walk each step from here.

Please reach out to me at **hello@michellekeating.com** – I'd love to hear how you're going, what you learn, experience and achieve along the way.

For ongoing inspiration on your journey, sign up to my newsletter at michellekeating.com

Acknowledgements

Thank you to everyone who supported me as I brought this book to life. It hasn't been an easy journey. I learned so much about myself and the process along the way and I am incredibly grateful to the people who stuck by my side to see it through and help it Shine!

Thank you to Leesa Ellis from 3 Ferns <3ferns.com>. Your expertise, generosity and patience is greatly appreciated. Katie Rickson <katierickson.co.nz>, thank you for picking up the pieces of my first draft and bringing it to life with your trademark wit and wisdom. Christine Sheehy <bookcoach.co.nz>, thank you for helping me with the final polishing of my story and manuscript.

To Kristina Karlsson and Paul Lacy, for everything you created with kikki.K and the Dream Life movement. Your stores gave me the courage to dream and reach for the stars. My time working alongside you was magic in so many ways. That dream may have come to an end but the ripples from it will last forever in so many ways around the world. Keep dreaming big!

To Sophie, Carly, Kelly, Megs, Greg, Frances, Arkie, Katie, Paige, Pip, Adhi, Ross and Rob for holding space for me and helping me cross the finish line of getting the manuscript finalised. I could not have walked those final miles without you.

To my journal testers: Angela, Dee, Jen, Kate, Kath and Pauline. I appreciate you taking the time to review the (very) rough draft and add your own ideas and sparkle to help shape the final product. I can't wait to share the final outcome with you!

To my Mum, Dad and sister Anna. Thank you for your support before, during and after my leap. Your generosity, belief and patience has allowed me to grow in ways I couldn't have previously imagined were possible.

To the incredible dreamers within the Dreamers Collective community. Thank you for believing in me when the world was falling apart. My world is a better place because of you.

To those who crossed my path and helped me find my inner sparkle and everyone who went before me, many of whom I have mentioned within these pages. You shined your lights so brightly they helped me find my way in the dark.

And finally, to you the reader, thank you for picking up this book. The belief that someone's life would be made better by me making this dream a reality kept me going when things got hard and life got in the way. Thank you for having the courage to listen to that small voice within, I cannot wait to hear where it leads you.

Thank you for being you xxx

About the author

MICHELLE KEATING

In 2013, Michelle felt stuck and alone. After her second attempt at business hadn't gone to plan, she resigned herself to being in a 9 to 5 job for the rest of her life.

But something didn't feel right.

She longed for something different and couldn't shake the feeling that she was meant to do more with her life.

Shine is Michelle's story of letting go of her steady job, and chasing her dream to do work she loved, which led to her presenting over 500 workshops for global stationery brand kikki.K, speaking at and hosting multiple live events and founding Dreamers Collective, an online community that helps women follow through on their big dreams.

She is on a mission to inspire others to connect with their uniqueness within – their inner sparkle, so they can design and live a life they love and make a difference in the world.

When she's not chasing dreams, you'll find her writing in her journal, mixing up a cocktail, tending to her flower garden, or admiring the sunrise or sunset from her home by the beach.

Michelle lives in Auckland, New Zealand with her husband Rob and their much-loved daughter Grace.

Stay connected with Michelle at
michellekeating.com

◎ _michellekeating_

◎ dreamers.collective.co

www.ingramcontent.com/pod-product-compliance
Lightning Source LLC
Chambersburg PA
CBHW051546010526
44118CB00022B/2598